D0886615

A Temporary Sort of Peace

A Memoir of Vietnam

A Temporary Sort of Peace

A Memoir of Vietnam

Jim McGarrah

Indiana Historical Society Press
Indianapolis 2007

This book is a publication of the
Indiana Historical Society Press
450 West Ohio Street
Indianapolis, Indiana 46202-3269 USA
www.indianahistory.org

Telephone orders 1-800-447-1830
Fax orders 317-234-0562
Online orders at http://shop.indianahistory.org

Library of Congress Cataloging-in-Publication Data

McGarrah, Jim, 1948-
   A temporary sort of peace : a memoir of Vietnam / James McGarrah.
      p. cm.
   ISBN 978-0-87195-258-5 (cloth : alk. paper) 1. McGarrah, Jim, 1948-
2. Vietnam War, 1961-1975—Personal narratives, American. 3. Soldiers—
Indiana—Biography. 4. United States. Marine Corps—Biography. I. Title.
   DS559.5.M414 2007
   959.704'3092—dc22
   [B]

                                    2007010528

Printed in Canada

This book is dedicated to Leslie and John and their generation in the hopes that one day history will quit repeating itself, and to the memory of Joe Sayyah and Jim Hayes, brothers-in-arms and casualties of the Vietnam War many years later.

CONTENTS

ACKNOWLEDGMENTS

The following personal narrative is as accurate as my memory allows. Some of the names have been changed intentionally to protect the innocent and the not so innocent.

Thanks to *Southern Indiana Review* for publishing "Dead Reckoning: A Treaty of the Mind," to *Under the Sun* for publishing "Cahn Cho," and to *Elixir Magazine* for publishing "Blind Barber" and "Hot Toddy."

Thanks to the Faculty Research and Creative Work Award committee at the University of Southern Indiana for financing my return to Vietnam so I could write the epilogue.

Thanks to good friends who read either part or all of the early drafts and gave me honest advice and helpful suggestions: Patty Aakhus, Matthew Graham, Susan McCarty, Ron Mitchell, Leslie Ullman, Heidi Weaver, and Tom Wilhelmus.

Thanks to my son, John, for taking the photographs featured in the epilogue.

Thanks to the Indiana Historical Society Press for taking a chance.

Chapter 1

DEAD RECKONING: A TREATY OF THE MIND

Back home again in Evansville, Indiana, I'm locking my car. My conscious mind says there's really no need for locks in this neighborhood in broad daylight. During my high school years, I never took the keys out of the ignition and my mother never locked the front door of our house. But that was thirty years ago, a whole other lifetime. Something deep inside me is afraid now. I turn and walk across the asphalt parking lot of the Veterans' Administration Outpatient Clinic on Walnut Street. Three old warriors of some past conflict pick up litter with the same tentative motions, as if thinking about each stoop and each lift represents a collective and unbearable burden. They are six arms and six legs linked to one common incubus of monotony. They nod at me in unison, as if each can read my thoughts.

The electric door opens with my footstep, pushing the overcast sky away and replacing it with the fluorescent smile of a file clerk. As the door closes behind me with a hydraulic hiss, I flinch. It has the exact same sound as a tab top popping on a Pepsi can or a bolt going home on an M-16 rifle.

"Can I help you?"

"I have an appointment in mental health."

"Mr. McGarrah, service connected disability. I have your paperwork. Go on in and have a nice day. They're waiting for you."

I appreciate this man's hospitality and his attempt to make the VA user friendly. It reminds me of an article I read in my morning newspaper about the current effort by the Missouri Ku Klux Klan to join the Adopt-A-Highway program. Image is everything, isn't it? Still, it's difficult to reconcile the file clerk's southern Indiana friendliness with the idea that someone behind closed doors will soon be dissecting my brain for broken parts with the same attitude, or even with sincerity.

For the first twenty-five years after the Vietnam War ended the VA dealt with us veterans of the war as if we were illegal aliens in an overcrowded barrio. As long as we kept hiding, we could receive the leftover benefits of the legitimate veterans who fought in the *good* wars. As long as we were silent and didn't remind the nation how much a mistake costs, we could be treated with semi-benevolent condescension and with no great sacrifice.

Now, Vietnam-era veterans are showing up in universities, practicing law and medicine, serving in Congress, and even running for president. Our scars are visible outside the walls of our homes. Frustration and confusion have replaced our guilt. Our questions are being articulated loudly and with intelligence. Consequently, the VA's health service has been forced to reinvent itself as a caring, nurturing, all-encompassing Health Maintenance Organization. I like the idea, but, if you believe Plato, only the idea can be true.

Even with the visible changes such as bright pastoral reproductions on the walls, buffed floors, and free coffee making me suspicious, I take a seat in the waiting room and rummage through the wrinkled copies of *Reader's Digest.* No matter how much fresh paint alters the surface appearance of this place, the smell of dying men still clings to the air.

What powerful sensations the olfactory system provides. It can excite you—the scent of a lonely woman in a crowded bar or the fragrance of an untried exotic dish in a new restaurant. It can soothe you—the hint of alfalfa after a spring rain or the aroma of French Market coffee in the early morning. The nose will also terrify—the stench of diesel fuel as you hurry to beat a train or the hint of someone else's aftershave on your wife's pillowcase.

Sometimes, like now, as I sit on a vinyl couch next to an old man with yellow skin and watch him pick lint from a dirty sweater, the sense of smell can open a pathway from the present to the past. It acts as a conduit carrying the stench from where it is back to where it has been. I'm smelling unwashed clothes and rotting flesh in this VA clinic. Instantly, the autumn outside the doors is just a multicolored dream of maple trees, baseball tournaments, and freckled girls tied like helium balloons to the arms of future farmers.

Someone is gurgling on my right. I rip the cellophane from a pack of Marlboros and slap it across a hole in a chest. The chest and the hole belong to a man named Tri. We're in a dry ditch. A wall of tracer fire from several AK-47s traps us there. The cellophane sucks into the hole, creates a vacuum and stops his lung from collapsing, but blood still seeps around the edges. Where's my damn pressure bandage?

"Jim. Jim. . . . Mr. McGarrah, sir. Excuse me. My name is Tom. Follow me, please. What made you come visit us after thirty years?"

"Well, Tom, I got a Xeroxed letter from your regional director. She said the VA really cares about me now. I think I might be a little depressed, too. A man I trust says I have those symptoms."

"Why do you trust him? Is he a doctor?"

"No. He's a Vietnam veteran."

Tom begins to write my history, speaking rapidly as he writes. His head is bowed and the words from his lips seem to roll down his arm and off the pen. He has a huge caseload and needs me to stick with the facts because time is a valuable commodity in a world filled with case numbers and stereotypes. There is no more time in life for substance, just time for forms. Do I have nightmares?

3

Only when I sleep. Do I drink? Only before dinner and sometimes after. Have I ever used drugs? I went to college, the first time, in the 1960s. Why'd he even have to ask that question?

It was then I realized what kind of picture Tom was drawing of my life. To me it seemed more like a caricature, a hyperbolic picture of a person I knew well but was not close to. This person was a poly-drug abuser and an alcoholic with a sleep disorder who feared intimacy. Surely it was not fear that pushed me in and out of four marriages like an electric spark shoots through a hot wire? Why did he ask me if I was uncomfortable being intimate with people? I had been intimate with a lot of people.

I hear the click and static of a PRC 25 radio. "Foxfire one . . . foxfire one . . . this is one Charlie niner. I have one Whiskey India Alpha and one Kilo India Alpha. Request immediate medivac . . . over."

"One Charlie niner . . . this is foxfire one. LZ too hot . . . cannot respond. Do you copy . . . over?" The wall of lead has moved forward at least a hundred meters. The squad leader rushes up to my point position, stands over me and packs white gauze into the cavity under my knee. I see splintered bone. My left shoulder tingles. Warm liquid runs down my arm, dripping off numb fingers. The blood soaks into the dirt and irrigates the elephant grass. I'm looking at the arm and leg, but there is no pain. These strange appendages seem to belong to another creature. Pain is a thief in the night. It never comes while you're watching.

The squad leader is smiling like a high school quarterback after scoring with the homecoming queen. He says that Tri and I did a fine job uncovering the enemy ambush. Judging from a few bodies they were forced to leave behind, these men were North Vietnamese Army regulars moving toward Hue for the Tet Offensive. If we had not engaged them, their automatic weapons would have cut apart the next truck convoy coming down Highway 1. He takes the cellophane off of my best friend's chest. The gurgling has stopped. Can his wife grow rice alone?

Tom's hypnotic baritone makes me wonder why I want to go back. Isn't that really what this is all about? If I want to go forward, I have to go back. Ion Eremia, a Romanian political prisoner, once wrote, "You must not silence that voice within you that is crying to be heard, or, as you yourself sense, there will always be a part of you that will remain unfulfilled." I need to hear my own voice again, the one that tells me who I am and who I might become. I have to go back to where it was lost in order to find it.

"Jim, you seem to be exhibiting some symptoms of post-traumatic stress disorder, or PTSD, as it's sometimes called. Have you ever considered the possibility that you have this? It's very common with men who've seen as much combat as you have. Do you ever have intrusive thoughts about the war?"

Triage is crowded. It is late in the afternoon when I arrive at the Phu Bai MASH for emergency surgery and the wounded pile up quickly in war. Eighteen days into the 1968 Tet Offensive, and here I lie with tubes running in and out of several jagged holes in my flesh. I watch the doctor scrub his hands quickly over a stainless-steel sink and move down the assembly line of operating tables to the one next to mine. The water dripping from the hands is pink with someone's blood. A masked nurse tells me to close my eyes and travel back home, back home again to Indiana. I close my eyes and look for cornfields and John Deere tractors, 1957 Chevys and blond cheerleaders wearing angora wrapped class rings, 4-H livestock shows and watermelon festivals, strip pits and deer, county courthouses and A&W root beer. I try. I really try. But in the dark behind my eyes, colors explode, vague shapes surround me, slowing down my travel. I only get as far as a few miles and a few minutes ago. I'm bouncing in the back of a truck loaded with still-warm bodies from the Second Battalion, Fifth Marine Division, in a fierce firefight south of the Perfume River in Hue. The CH-46D was too big a target. You can't risk losing a whole helicopter and crew just to medivac one live marine. So, the corpsman throws me on the first passing vehicle headed south, and this is it. If I die en route, I'm already moving toward the morgue with my companions. Semper Fidelis.

"Tom, is it possible to be a nineteen-year-old boy and fight in a war, *any war*, ten thousand miles from home, and not end up with intrusive thoughts every day thereafter? You're the expert Tom. What's the answer? Is it possible to fight in a war and not have PTSD?"

My voice is rising and my new therapist smiles an all-knowing smile. He doesn't seem to be condescending. I feel his struggle for empathy. Nevertheless, I also feel a real urge for a shot of Jim Beam and maybe just two or three beers. More than that, I want to leave this smell behind. This odor of old, tired men started these memories today. This aroma of unfulfilled dreams and unrequited conscience and unresolved conflict keeps nauseating me because I'm not sure it's on the outside coming in. What if it's inside and rising up?

Am I simply another addition to the caseload? I look around the waiting room as I rush from Tom's office on my way out. All of these men I see are struggling just to catch a breath. Some are homeless. Some are helpless. How did I wake up inside their nightmares? I've been where they've been. Must I go where they're going as an act of contrition?

It's cooler now, in the parking lot. A light drizzle sifts through the thick air like wet sand and sticks to my skin. The three old warriors laugh and light cigarettes in unison. The trash is retrieved.

"Where ya goin' on this fine day?" the fattest one asks.

"I'm goin' to a school to teach poetry. I just started my second lifetime."

"Well, I hope it turns out better than the first."

His eyes seem to glaze over slightly as he picks up his trash bag and limps toward the dumpster.

In the car, Bob Edwards is on the radio. National Public Radio's *Morning Edition* is doing a feature on the tourist industry in Vietnam, "the emerald jewel of Southeast Asia," and America's new partner in commerce. It seems that the Marriott and Sheraton hotel chains are concerned about profit and overhead. The monsoons have slowed construction on their new resorts, creating cost overruns. Even the Hilton in Hanoi can't keep its rooms full during the monsoons.

I knew another Hilton in Hanoi as a young man. It was always full. But, as a young man, I also learned that monsoons were rainstorms. For three decades, my one sane point of mental convergence focused on the assurance that these hard rains would fall every year in absolution and eventually wash the blood from the canvas of my dreams. Today, Bob Edwards sets me straight. Monsoons have never been what I thought they were. I always equated them with the southern Indiana thunderstorms the old farmers from Gibson County call "toad stranglers" because here, my home, was my only frame of reference. I was wrong. Monsoons are without substance, just seasonal shifts in upper air wind direction. They are simply forms of air that carry the rain inland from the Gulf of Tonkin.

A calm settles over me as I turn west on the expressway. My first class at the university begins in fifteen minutes. Listening to the raindrops dodge the wipers, I think I might really keep this teaching job. I think that maybe I can finish at least one thing I've started and started and started. After all, I'm finally fifty years old and have become a semiresponsible family man. Most importantly, I'm beginning to see my life as more than illusion. It is a pastiche of imagination, substance, and passionate ideas that my memory has allowed me to step in and out of at random, but not without context and meaning. Today is the day I realize that a monsoon is just wind.

Chapter 2

HOT TODDY

When I was nine years old in 1957 I learned to equate survival with drinking. This connection between good whiskey and life continued through my tour of duty in Vietnam and continues today under the psychobabble label of "self medication." It's amazing to me that circumstance determines how people view the exact same liquid substance with either appreciation or loathing. If my family had been Fundamental Christians in those days instead of fundamentally prosperous and middle-class Americans, I might well have died from a curable disease.

We lived at 514 West Broadway in Princeton, Indiana. A huge white house with a wraparound antebellum-type porch complete with Roman columns, it was built in the nineteenth century and, back then, was a centerpiece on the main street of town. A magnolia tree, one of the few in southern Indiana, grew majestically on the east lawn, and directly across the street the American Legion Home reminded us that we were an all-American family in an all-American neighborhood.

Consequently, one of the first things I faced when I woke up every morning, besides the pear tree outside my bedroom window on the west side of the house, was a huge American flag flapping on the pole across the street. It was not unusual for me to sit up in bed, rub my eyes, and see red. On this particular morning, though, the red floated before me in dots, not stripes.

"Mom, I'm hot. My throat hurts. Everything is red."

"I'll be there in a minute, I'm peeling potatoes," my mother yelled from the kitchen. "Don't wake your sister."

"Mom. MOM. I'm hungry," shouted Sandy, my six-year-old sister, from her room.

"I just told you not to wake your sister."

"I didn't."

My mother appeared in the doorway drying her hands on a dishtowel and gave me the look that meant she was pretending to be angry, but really glad to be distracted from the banality of peeling potatoes.

"Your father's at work and I was in the kitchen. So if not you, then who?"

"I don't know."

Sandy shuffled into the room dragging a dirty, stuffed, bald-headed doll she had labeled Donna for reasons unknown to everyone but her.

"I'm still hungry."

"Of course you are. Go in the kitchen and sit down at the breakfast nook while I feel your brother's forehead."

Crossing the room, my mother laid the back of her porcelain white hand on my skin. It felt cool and reassuring until she spoke.

"My goodness, you're on fire."

"Where?" I said, and, panic-stricken, began flailing my arms.

"No, I mean you have a fever. Do you still see red dots?"

"No, but I might be wearing invisible red glasses because now everything is red."

"Open your mouth."

Like the hungry little blue jay nesting in the pear tree, I opened as wide as I could while my mother left the room and returned with a flashlight and a thermometer. She swirled the beam of light around my throat and shook the mercury down in the glass tube.

"Put this under your tongue and don't talk."

"HighcatItuck."

"You can't talk because then I can't take your temperature."

Within minutes, I discovered that my temperature had risen from the normal 98.6 degrees Fahrenheit to 102.5 degrees, a number my mother didn't seem pleased with. She told me to stay in bed and she would bring me an aspirin dissolved in Coca-Cola for the fever and a glass of warm salt water to gargle for my throat. I heard my sister clanging silverware in the kitchen as I returned my head to the pillow. Now that I knew I had a fever, I felt very ill.

In the Eisenhower years, when all white, middle-class families pretended to have perfectly happy lives, it was normal for doctors to make house calls, more than normal, expected. I heard my mother on the telephone talking with Doctor Peck, our family physician who supposedly had courted her during high-school days before she met my father.

"It's over 102. Yes. No, not yet. The measles? Where are the spots? Can you come over later today and take a look? Thanks."

Returning to my room with what I considered a treat, a Coke for breakfast, she sat on the edge of the bed and gave me an anxious stare.

"Doc Peck says the measles are going around and with your sore throat and fever and the red tint in your sight, you've probably got them. He's coming by this afternoon. Till then you are to remain quiet and stay in the dark."

I swallowed the cold soda. The taste was sullied by the grainy, bitter, ground-up tablet, but I forced it down hoping for a plain refill, and I got one for being a good boy.

In those days, I wasn't accustomed to the boredom that seems to infect my twenty-first-century children. Even sick days held the promise of adventure. I slipped out of my bed after Mom returned to the kitchen to feed Sandy and hurried to the far north corner of our huge house. In the small room beyond my parents' bedroom sat our family's prize possession, a Zenith console television. Keeping the volume as low as possible, I turned it on to my favorite program, *The Pinky Lee Show*. With a black-and-white television, however, it was virtually out of the question for me to understand why the man in the funny hat who danced around trees and blew up balloons would be named Pinky.

"James Earl, I hear the TV. I'm not deaf yet." Another prophecy to be fulfilled at a later date. In her waning years, my mother did go deaf due to nerve damage from consuming thousands of aspirin tablets to quell the horrific pain of her migraines, which seemed to occur in direct proportion to my father's misadventures with alcohol.

"It's Pinky Lee." Pain shot through my throat. I felt light-headed and like I might burn up at any given minute.

"Get back to bed and don't strain your eyes anymore."

* * *

Doctor Peck arrived at lunch. My sister led him to my room while she munched the last of a grilled-cheese sandwich.

"You're gonna get a shot now," she said.

"Sandy, we don't know that," said my mother, trailing the doctor. "You go watch cartoons. I'll call if we need you."

"Promise. I want to see."

I had spent my whole life around Doc Peck. He brought me into the world, gave me all of my childhood inoculations followed by grape Tootsie Roll Pops, and prescribed horrible, chalky tasting liquid penicillin that fooled me the first time I took it because it was the color of bubble gum. He set my first of fifteen broken bones and never treated me with anything but kindness. And yet, every time he walked into the room, he terrified me with his pres-

12

ence. I couldn't get past it. Maybe it was the idea that I never saw him unless I was sick or needed something that would hurt. Maybe his six-foot-four-inch frame and freckled complexion topped with thinning red hair reminded me of a giant Howdy Doody, that strange TV puppet who spoke in fragmented sentences. Howdy Doody was one scary puppet locked inside a television. God forbid he should come to life and be allowed to poke me with needles in the sanctity of my bedroom.

More than anything, I think Doc's voice is what always set me on edge. The words seemed to hum from his nose with the sound of an electric razor and that made him seem more alien than human. I had seen *Invasion of the Body Snatchers* and, as if that wasn't bad enough, *The Blob*. My mother said he had adenoids. Of course, I later learned that everyone has adenoids, but they don't filter language through them. Armed with that knowledge, I became even more suspicious.

Doc Peck set his black bag on the floor and sat on the edge of my bed. The bag opened from the top and the sides had compartments in them filled with various and sundry tools of the medical trade. Of all the shiny steel objects and glass vials, the thing I dreaded the most was an innocuous-looking giant wooden Popsicle stick called a tongue depressor, and it was the first object he extracted.

"Open wide young man," he buzzed, and pressed my tongue down with the dry wood. "Wider."

He slid the wood further back on my tongue and with his free hand brought a penlight up to my mouth, shining the beam down the dark cavern of my throat. "Wider."

I gagged and felt as if I might choke to death. The more I gagged the further he pushed in the wooden stick. My tongue, the only defense I had against this invasion, wrestled with the foreign object, but the stick seemed to have a life of its own and slipped from every hold. Just as I reached my hands up to push his hand away, he pulled the thing out and broke it in half, handing it to my mother to throw into the trash. My eyes had clouded with tears.

"Now, that wasn't so bad, was it?" Whenever an adult says that to a child, it is an act of contrition. The adult is honestly acknowledging that the child has just been tortured and is begging forgiveness on the off chance the child grows up to become a serial killer looking for revenge. "And besides, men don't cry. What if your sister saw you?"

The rest of the exam passed swiftly and without discomfort. He listened to my heart through his stethoscope, and then allowed me the same privilege. The sound reminded me of old radio special effects, the way some man in a studio re-created the echo of hoofbeats by thumping halved coconut shells against a plywood board. In those days, I often pictured my heart as a coconut.

Perhaps the image was the way I chose to deal with what I couldn't possibly understand—death. By creating an illusion of an illusion, I had a buffer to keep me from dwelling on the fact that if the sound of my heart stopped, so did I. This particular survival technique served me well years later when I went to war. By pretending my body was something other than flesh, often a combination of celluloid and movie star, I could quickly dispel the nausea that sometimes came when people around me were blown to bits. John Wayne, Audie Murphy, Steve Reeves, and Johnny Weismueller all overcame horrific obstacles on screen and lived to make more movies with even worse travails.

"Come over here, Juanita." My mother stepped up to the bed. The doctor had his fingers pressed against the side of my neck. "His glands are swollen and his throat is inflamed. Open up, Jimmy." I did reluctantly, afraid the tongue depressor might reappear. Instead, it was a beam of light. "See those red patches on the roof of his mouth? It's the measles, alright."

"Where are the spots on the rest of him?" My mother wrung her hands.

Doc closed his bag with a frightening finality and stood, tilting his head sideways twice for her to follow him down the hallway out of earshot. As the adults left, Sandy poked her head around the corner.

"Did you get a shot?"

"No, not even any medicine."

"Faker."

"Am not. I've got measles."

"So what. I've got a birthmark *and* a weak eye."

The door at the end of the hallway closed as the doctor left and my mother came charging back down the hall.

"Sandy, I told you to watch TV. Leave your brother alone. He's contagious."

*   *   *

Two days and nights went by. I remained isolated and in the dark. My father poked his head in occasionally during the evenings when he came home from work and brought me juice and toast in the mornings before he left. Weakness made him uncomfortable. On the morning of the third day, I knew my condition was serious because he brought me a new Rawlings baseball glove and a can of neat's-foot oil. My father tried to cheer me up when he felt the circumstances dire. Minor traumas were lessons in life that required manly discipline, not sentimentality. Actual kindness in our family was reserved for death, old women, and the less fortunate unrelated to us. The expensive glove could only mean pneumonia, brain tumor, or some disease that required an enema.

"This'll give you something constructive to do while you're sick. You've got time to break the glove in, and men always need to be doing something constructive. Pour the oil in the pocket and rub it slowly around then up over the fingers, like this." He slowly followed his own instructions till the puddle of liquid in the center of the glove soaked into the hungry leather, turning it from a light gold color to a deep chocolate.

I trusted my father's baseball advice. He had signed a professional contract right out of high school and played for a short time in the Canadian League. In 1941 he voluntarily ended any dream he had of pitching in the majors by joining the army. After three years of combat, two wounds, and a bronze star with the Eighty-second Airborne in Europe, he came home tired and cleansed of any need to compete on a field of honor.

Taking the glove from his hand and working the oil, I yelled "Thanks Dad" at the back of his head. We had just come as close as we would for the next two decades to bonding, and it felt good. I massaged the oil into the leather for what seemed a long time. The smell of neat's-foot and new leather comforted me, and still does to this day.

I wasn't hungry, but could tell by the rustling in the kitchen that it must have been getting close to lunchtime. My mother entered the bedroom with a glass full of what looked like dishwater.

"Time for you to drink this."

"What is it?"

"It's called a hot toddy and the doctor says it's the only thing that can help you."

"Help me what?"

"Get well."

"I'm feeling a lot better."

"Look at your arm and tell me what you don't see."

I studied the tan skin, the light brown fuzz, a mole, and the blue veins on the back of my hand. "It looks like it always does."

"Exactly, and measles have spots. Your body should be covered with red spots. Doc Peck says if this doesn't bring them out today we're going to have to take you to the hospital. Measles that don't break out can cause you to get really, really sick."

"What's in it?"

"Some lemon and sugar and hot water and a magical ingredient compliments of your father."

Frightened by the prospect of being locked up in a hospital where people die, I took the glass from my mother and downed it quickly. There was a strong hint of wood smoke and a bitter aftertaste, but the pain in my throat subsided almost immediately. I began to feel slightly numb, but mom said that was normal. A permanent condition of my father's, she said. She read me a few pages from a library book about the life of Ty Cobb, my baseball idol because he slid into bases spikes high and took shit from no one, and I began to get drowsy.

"I want to be the Indiana Peach."

"I think there was only one peach and he was the Georgia Peach. But you could be an Indiana Sycamore. How about that?"

"Is an Indiana Sycamore tough?"

"Tough enough for you."

* * *

Grandma sings: I'll cling to the old rugged cross and exchange it someday for a crown. The air trembles as I slip under to be purged by holy hands pushing down on my chest. I struggle, but the cold water swallows me. Demonic voices bubble: "Count backward from one hundred." There's been a mistake. I'm supposed to be saved. Fluorescent clouds roll toward me, their whiteness swirling like gauze. I hear the liturgy chanted in beeps and pings. The eyes of the congregation snake inside me, slice my flesh, and expose my sin, which pours out of me in round dots. I can't see, hear, or feel anything except rushing water behind my ears, an indiscriminate force freed of form and structure by its own nature. Like spilled neat's-foot oil an ache creeps from my chest to my head. I am resurrected, an old man who looks like Jesus. Water mixes with wine in the slow seep of leather-stitched fingers. There are strange angels in ball caps whose hands reek of isopropyl and disease.

I awoke at dusk terrified. It was that limbo time when you're between the light and the dark, the purgatory of the day. My body was bright red and the sheets were soaked as if a dam had broken inside me and a river of tiny strawberries poured out. Sweat leaked from my forehead.

"Mom," I screamed. "It worked. The magic worked."

My mother, sister, and father all hurried into my room from various parts of the house. My father's face lit up with a huge smile.

"Well, I'll be damned. Juanita, don't you ever complain about the cabinet being full of Jim Beam again. Saved this boy's life, it did. What don't kill you makes you stronger. That's what a real man knows." Catching my mother's grimace from the corner of his eye, Dad quickly amended his statement. "In moderation, of course. It won't kill you in moderation."

My mother shook her head and sat down on the bed, wiping my face with a wet cloth. My sister brought her doll, Donna, over to stare at me with vacant glass eyes.

"See, Donna? I told you he'd look stupid."

The author in his Princeton Little League all-star uniform, 1960.

Chapter 3

SLIPPERY WHEN WET

Most white, middle-class, baby boomer American men, if given time away from the business of being an inherently, but often unintentionally, arrogant, Eurocentric, macho elitist, can remember countless circumstances when that attitude was seeded through pain in their childhood psyches. One stands out clearly in my mind.

A few short years after I recovered from the measles, I caught another horrible disease, one that my mother referred to snidely as "the bane of her existence," called puberty. One symptom of this illness constantly resurfaced, first on the baseball field and later at every opportunity, the need to prove that, even though much shorter in stature than my father, I was still going to be the better *man* and outdo what my father had done. As it turns out, this may have been one of the primary reasons, though certainly not the only one, I joined the Marine Corps and went to Vietnam. The ability to fight your own war often becomes a rite of passage in the American male psyche and a driving force behind many stupid decisions.

The McGarrah males had a long history of fighting the good fight, from the Civil War forward. All I thought when my father argued violently to keep me from enlisting was that he must be jealous because his war was over and I might win more medals in mine. I don't think I ever considered he had learned through experience that the word *man* was just the back half of the more important word *human*, or that being a better human rather than a better man might be a loftier and more beneficial goal. And perhaps, while he was responsible to a certain degree for the chip on my shoulder, he certainly wasn't for my choices because he often gave me ambivalent advice, especially on the baseball field where I spent most of my time from the ages of eight through eighteen.

The year I graduated from Little League to Babe Ruth League and from rubber spikes to metal ones is a good example.

"Don't forget what Leo Durocher said about nice guys, son."

"They finish last."

"Exactly."

Dad was fond of that catchphrase, as he was of many others, but it caused some guilt. If I played the game tough, aggressive, mean, and hard, as Leo the famous manager of the Brooklyn Dodgers felt all good baseball players should, then it occasionally generated questionable behavior for a thirteen-year-old shortstop in the Babe Ruth League. Mothers of other players tended to scream and cry when I sliced their sons' legs open by sliding into second base spikes high to break up a double play, or split a lip by tagging someone directly with the baseball. At this point my father would forget that all the other fathers of his generation were giving their sons the same advice. He would be overwhelmed with humanity and chant off another of his favorite proverbs from the dugout. "Son, when the one great scorer comes to write against your name, he writes not that you won or lost, but how you played the game."

I spent years trying to decipher and live the dichotomy between tough son of a bitch and sensitive man, between win at all costs but play fair doing it. There were times in the jungles of Vietnam that the hesitation between these two extremes almost cost me my life. On a particular day at Southside Baseball Field, I was about to learn my dad's most sincere understanding of the masculine role in society. A real man is toughest on himself. He may or may not show mercy to an enemy, but he asks no quarter, feels no pain, and sheds no tear when things don't go his way.

The author stands at the far left of the front row with his father, the team's coach, standing behind him, 1962.

It stormed off and on all morning, the summer wind blowing up one toad strangler after another until the ball field was awash in a beige soup of dirt and water. But it was mid-July and the league standings were on the line, so the weather had to be conquered and the game played. Fathers from both teams raked, scraped, and swept puddles from the infield. In the worst spots around first and third base, some piled old tires, soaked them with gasoline and burned them. Black smoke rose from the diamond-shaped altar to the god of baseball and summer. Slowly, the blue and orange flames ate the pools of rain.

After each team circled, held hands, and prayed for the complete destruction of the other by divine intervention and blood, we took the field thirty minutes late at 2 p.m. The sun roared out from behind the clouds, steam rose from our uniforms, and the air we breathed choked the back of our throats like thick burritos soaked with habanero sauce. We played with the fire that only the righteous innocent can manage, the lead seesawing back and forth between teams from inning to inning until the last one when the game was tied at three runs apiece. We had won the toss and chosen to bat last. Three outs away from extra innings, I stood in the left batter's box, pawing the dirt with my spikes to secure my back foot, tapping the plate three times with my bat, cocking my left elbow high, and leaning forward slightly, knees bent.

The opposing pitcher was as testosterone driven as me. We were at war, man to man, and only one would survive as victor. His name was John. Taller and heavier than most of the other players in the league, he led the league in strikeouts with a wicked fastball. When he was on, my dad used to say, "John's throwing aspirin tablets." And he had been *on* all day. The first pitch ran in and brushed me back away from the plate. John smiled. The bastard had tried to scare me, so I crowded the plate even more. The second pitch roared by high and away. I had run the count to two balls and no strikes. John was tired and couldn't afford to walk me. I believed he would take some steam off of his next pitch simply to make sure it was over the plate. He did. I swung and got the middle of the bat where the wood starts to narrow on the ball. A looping fly lofted over the first baseman's head and dropped just inside the right field foul line. I was on first with a single.

The next batter hit a pop-up to third. With one out, I stole second. The next hitter grounded to the shortstop. The shortstop hesitated on his throw, trying to hold me on second. When he did finally let the ball go to first, I dug in and ran to third. His throw barely nipped the batter at first for the second out. Now I was on third with two outs in the bottom of the last inning and the score tied. Even though our cleanup hitter was at bat, he had caused John no trouble all day, striking out three times. My father stood in the coaching box on the third base line.

"This is it," he whispered.

"Billy hasn't touched the ball all day."

"I know that, but I think you've got a shot to steal home. The pitcher is taking a full windup instead of throwing from the stretch. But if you do, make sure you slide."

"You make sure Billy gets the signal. I don't want a bat in my teeth."

It was a bold move, a manly one. I could see my dad's wisdom. John was stepping on the pitcher's mound and facing the batter. When he got ready, he would crank his arms like a windmill, kick his left leg high in the air, step toward home plate, and release the ball, completely ignoring the base runner (me) at third. This was the common practice for a pitcher because the need to hold the runner close to the base diminished greatly once that runner reached this point. No one in his right mind believed he could outrun a fastball to home plate. So, no one bothered to try and steal home. What made the idea possible in John's case was the fact that he always hesitated at the top of his windup and took a long time to finally release the ball. In my short, piston-like legs I held the power of a quick start. My father knew I would be halfway down the baseline before John's pitch.

His hands went up and he signaled to the umpire for a time-out. Calling Billy out of the batter's box, he met him and whispered something in his ear. I assumed he told Billy to take the first pitch, or fake a bunt, or something other than swing the bat in my face. That was a message too important to trust to hand signals. On the way back to the coaching box, Dad touched the bill of his ball cap. The message had been delivered and received by all parties. John began his windup and I left the safety of third base behind, digging in and pushing off with each step down the line like a deer trying to outrun a headlight.

My peripheral vision caught the ball leaving his hand. The closer I got to home, the larger the white sphere grew in the corner of my eye. I seemed to be one side of a triangle, the ball the other. Boy and object were destined to intersect right over home plate. Billy stepped clear of the batter's box, and I went parallel to the earth. Sliding on my left side, I heard the ball pop into the catcher's mitt and, almost simultaneously, heard a second pop as if someone had broken a #2 pencil in math class. The umpire had his face mask in hand. He threw both arms out wide in a horizontal gesture I recognized. *Safe.* The run was in and we won the game. I was a hero covered with mud, sweat, and glory. Then the pain came.

At first, I couldn't believe anything hurt this bad. Not even strep throat, or the time I rode my tricycle off the curb and broke my front tooth at the gum line, rivaled the intense throb of hurt barreling up my leg at breakneck speed and smashing into my brain. The umpire stood over me and kept the other players back. My father ran down the baseline and joined him.

"You were safe, son. We won."

"My leg . . ."

"It's nothing, probably just a little sprain. Spit and throw some dirt on it. That's what my father used to tell me."

Doc Peck rushed onto the field from his seat in the stands and pushed through the crowd to kneel over me.

"Where's it hurt most?"

"He's fine," said my dad. "He's a tough kid, you know that."

Doc Peck must have known that because he didn't hesitate to torture me further by manipulating my knee and ankle until I screamed.

"Don't scream," Dad whispered. I stopped screaming.

Close to tears, I was bundled into the family car and driven to Gibson General Hospital, an ugly yellow and brown building on State Street with the word "Sanitarium" etched in stone above the doorway. Having made up my mind that I would die before uttering a word of discomfort, or shedding a single tear around my father, I lay on a gurney and stared at the tiled ceiling while the doctor took X-rays.

"John, his ankle's broke." Doc Peck said. "I'm going to need to set it and put it in a cast for at least eight weeks."

"Will it be healed by basketball season?"

"Shouldn't be a problem."

Soon, I was injected on and around the bone with Novocain, which guaranteed to eliminate the pain involved as Doc manipulated my ankle together so the healing would begin in a straight line along the fracture. Evidently, it had been a bad year for Novocain, or some pain can't be eliminated by numbness. I gripped the rails on the gurney and, white-knuckled, bit my lip till it bled. But there were no screams and no tears. I got used to dealing with life that way since this was the first of those fifteen bones broken over the years and since Doc didn't quite get the setting straight. In two weeks, I was sent to an orthopedic surgeon in Evansville named Lawrence who reset the break. He and I became good friends, first of all because he anesthetized me before breaking my ankle for the second time, but also because we constantly saw each other over the next few years as I returned for shoulder surgery to repair a football injury, hand surgery to straighten crippled fingers broken in a fistfight, and hand surgery again when Punkin' Lambert's slider pitch slid into my left wrist where I held the bat during the first inning of the regional American Legion baseball tournament in Evansville, Indiana.

I was eighteen then and played the rest of the game with a broken hand because my dad said there were college baseball scouts in the stands watching me. By the time the game reached the ninth inning, however, my hand had swelled so much it would barely fit into my glove. But Dad was right. I got an offer to play college ball.

In all fairness to my father, when he realized that my ankle had been broken and what it must have taken for me to remain silent and tearless that day when I stole home, guilt overtook him. For several weeks we went to amusement parks, zoos, major league baseball games, movies, and finally, Kentucky Lake for a holiday. His atonement was real and my sister and mother benefited from his generosity as well. By being hard on me first, Dad had broken his cardinal rule of manliness—"demand the most from yourself." By taking time away from business, from the horse races, from poker night, and from his Beefeater's gin to chauffeur us around and see that we were entertained, he could rest assured that the god of soldiers who survive war would absolve him from the sin of that survival.

Chapter 4

HOW DO I LOVE THEE?

Committing the mortal sin of every boy athlete, I fell in love for the first time with a cheerleader. If I considered myself a victim of life somehow, I might blame this fiasco on my sister. After all, she brought Katie home as if she were a lost puppy. However, I've never been a victim to much except my own devices. This time was no different. All learning begins with deconstruction, or in the case of teenage males, with humiliation. Long before Sandy brought her best friend to our house, I had made my decision that this girl was the *one*. I had no idea what being the one meant, but I knew her white, porcelain-smooth legs, long blonde hair, and the tiny, red cheerleader skirt that opened like a tulip to reveal her silk panties as she did her cartwheels, constricted my chest like a flattened squeeze box. That was enough to plunge forward in my quest.

By the time I met Katie, I was captain of the high school base-ball team and active participant on both the basketball and football teams. I had been selected, among other things, as the Optimist Club Youth of the Year and chosen "Personality Plus" by my senior classmates. My father, overwhelmed by my athletic achievements and community citations, bought me a 1957 Chevrolet Bel Air, which he paid to be painted canary yellow at my request, and which he had reupholstered with blue leather. The car was beautiful and, with its Holley four-barrel carburetor, could "shit and git," as my envious teammates used to say.

My point here is simple. As a popular senior in a small high school, a sophomore girl should have been falling all over herself climbing into the backseat of my car. Instead, I drove by her house in the south end of town on a regular basis long before my sister formally introduced us, hoping to catch a glimpse of her taking out the trash, walking the dog, or getting the mail. It was me who strategically placed himself by her locker at school when the bell rang to change classes, or found a table close to hers in the cafeteria. I drooled, fantasized, stuttered, and blushed my way through the first few months of 1966 until this cheerleader became a goddess in my mind before we ever spoke. I made her greater than the sum of her parts in my imagination and that was no one's fault but my own. When we finally went on a date, I had already been overwhelmed with who I wanted her to be for several months. Her apparent indifference to my advances only fueled my desire to have her completely and always that much more.

"I could go by the name James if I wanted to. It seems kind of stuck up to me."

"He's English," said Katie. "As an American, you don't have enough class for anything but Jim."

On screen at the Princeton Drive-In, Sean Connery introduced a new kind of hero to American males by whispering seductively in Ursula Andress' ear, "The name's Bond, James Bond." Gone was John Wayne's white horse. Gone was Randolph Scott's cocked hat. Gone was Audie Murphy standing in a field of dead Indians. Here was a killer who would actually get laid, a tough son of a bitch who knew how to talk a woman out of her panties. I scooted across the seat as suavely as I could in Bermuda shorts, the sweat from my thighs squeaking on the leather. Putting my arm around Katie as she leaned against the door in fright, I whispered gently, "The name's James . . ."

"I'm thirsty," she interrupted. "Would you get me a Coke from the concessions stand? Maybe some popcorn, too."

"Anything else?"

"Not yet. Hurry back."

Slump-shouldered and slack-jawed, I disappeared into the night to serve my goddess and her appetite.

As the year wore on, my grades dropped. I quit the basketball team to spend more time with Katie, which led her to be less enthusiastic during our less frequent make-out sessions. The more I did to be near her, the further she pulled away. It never dawned on me that she might feel pressured or controlled, even though I made all the decisions about what we ate, what movies we watched, where and when we made out.

I allowed Katie to shut me down if I went too far sexually, but I didn't appreciate her reticence or any possible reasons for it and always tried to go further during our next session. My father taught me never to be physically abusive with the weaker sex, and I obeyed my father because I wanted to be a good man and I thought that was how good men behaved. But, like most of the young men who reached puberty in the late 1950s and early 1960s, I learned that as a man I should take whatever action I desired initially and let the woman in my life react.

Depending on circumstance and reaction, the manly thing that followed most give and take like this was an act of semi-sincere contrition for going too far followed by a return to the status quo. A woman's feelings were yucky things to be tolerated as punishment for breaking God's laws and getting laid without making a baby.

As I got older and the 1960s wore on, I noticed women beginning to demand a measure of independence and more consideration from their males. Even my mother took a proactive stance and learned to remind my father whenever he got carried away—"I bring the bread home and by God, I'll do what I please"—that she deserved more respect.

Senior prom, 1966, Princeton High School.

One day after school during that senior year of 1966, I drove home from Katie's house where she and I had wrestled on the couch until her parents came in from work. So, it must have been around 5 p.m. as I entered the kitchen and heard Mom on the phone.

"What time will you be home?"

"Who's on the phone—Dad?"

"Supper will be ready in an hour and we aren't waiting." My mother cradled the phone and turned to me. "Go tell Sandy we're eating soon. You need to quit spending so much time over at Katie's."

"Why?"

"Because it isn't healthy."

That was my mother's way of reminding me that high school girls get knocked up by careless high school boys and then everyone's life is ruined forever. She would never consider talking with me about sexual intercourse, or even mention the word "sex." That area of responsibility belonged to my father, who had handled it with his customary aplomb four years earlier when I discovered a condom machine in the men's room of the bowling alley. As we were leaving, I asked him what condoms were for. "You mean 'cut rubbers.' Some men use them to prevent babies and some use them to prevent disease. As ugly as you are, the only use you'll have for them is just to blow them up and tie them on stop signs at Halloween. So, don't worry about it." That proved to be the only sex education talk I had with my father.

As mom had promised on the telephone earlier, we ate our supper this evening precisely at 6 p.m. and without my father. My mother cleared the table and began washing dishes with tears at the corner of her eyes. "Where's Dad?" Sandy asked. "I suspect he's still playing cards at the Elks Club." My mother's reply had a harsh ring to it. We knew enough to excuse ourselves and go watch *Gunsmoke* on TV before we caused my mother more aggravation with questions about Dad than he was causing by missing supper.

Sometime in the darkest part of night right before the dawn, the telephone rang in the kitchen. My mother got up and padded across the tile to answer. It proved to be my father, who had never returned home from his card game at the Elks. Calling from a casino in Las Vegas, he begged my mother's forgiveness, explaining that while he and his buddies played cards at the Elks they also drank a little too much and, at the time, it seemed like a good idea to charter a plane. Vegas *was* the very best place on earth to shoot craps and Dad believed he had found a lucky streak.

The next morning, Mom drove alone to the Evansville Regional Airport and collected my disheveled father from the return flight. I have no idea if he won or lost any money in Las Vegas. He never said. Also, for all his human flaws, my father tried to be an honest and decent man as he understood that honest and decent men should be. Consequently, he never gambled money from the family budget, or money that he couldn't afford to lose. He had built his automobile dealership up through the 1950s and it earned a tidy profit. We were part of the new and prosperous post-World War II midwestern middle class, and the family enjoyed those Eisenhower years, never wanting for anything materially. My father had a generous spirit and, in many ways, a kind heart. On the other hand, he seemed determined that some of his extra money that *he* had earned with his own hard work should be allotted to his personal entertainment, which consisted of Beefeater's gin and gambling.

I learned this sense of entitlement from him, part of which came from surviving combat, and carried it to troublesome extremes after Vietnam. The sins of the father are often compounded by the son.

Dad told me months later that my mother never spoke to him all the way home from the airport. In fact, I couldn't help but notice that she hardly spoke to him for the next two weeks, although he brought home flowers and candy on a regular basis. She had learned over the years to give as good as she got. My father hated salmon with a passion. He would rather eat dirt than fried salmon patties. For the two-week period of her silence and his repentance, Mom fixed salmon patties every night. The rest of us ate fried chicken, pork chops, and steak, but dad's plate was placed before him with two brown salmon patties and he didn't have the nerve to question the menu.

After I graduated in May 1966, I played my last summer season of American Legion baseball before going away. Katie had moved into her junior year of high school, and I wanted somehow to keep her at home and docile while I explored the big wide world of college. I had agreed to attend Kentucky Wesleyan, a small liberal arts school in Owensboro, Kentucky, and play baseball for the KWC Panthers. I felt excited and important when I picked Katie up and we drove to Gil Hodges Field for the afternoon American Legion game I was about to play. Some of the fathers, including mine, worked on the field as they had been doing since my childhood, lining the base paths and batters' boxes, raking the mound, and dragging the infield. I watched through the car windshield, amazed at how much energy these men expended to relive a little glory through their sons. The smell of vanilla on Katie's neck and the warmth of her leg pressed against mine distracted me. I was once again reminded that we had never gone "all the way."

Through the course of the past year, we spent a lot of time with each other and I had managed on several occasions to get her at least partially undressed. We had come as close to making love as I thought was possible without making love, but each time I began to penetrate her, she stopped me emphatically. I believed my restraint proved my love to her, and while it may have to some degree, it frustrated me completely. There were nights I came home from dates with enough rage to lift my car. The more this game went on, the more I began to feel as if she owed me her virginity and the more paranoid I became that someone else might get what belonged to me. My demands on her time and energy increased exponentially with her reticence. The goal was within my reach, but seemingly unattainable, an unsatisfactory paradox for any young male at this time in American history. The more intensely I demanded her affection, the more withdrawn she became and the angrier I got. This was our situation in the late summer American Legion baseball season of 1966 at Gil Hodges Field in Princeton, Indiana.

"You know I'm leaving for college in a few weeks."

"I know and I'll be wearing your class ring every day and I'll write you every day."

The senior ring I had given Katie months before rested securely on her wedding finger. With white angora yarn wrapped around the band to make it fit, the ring symbolized a pledge to her that I would date no college coeds. For me, it branded her with the symbol of my ownership. No pimply-faced high school punk would dare put a hand on this blonde-haired, blue-eyed beauty without running the risk of a most severe ass whipping.

"And I'll write you every day and call on the weekends and come home as much as I can."

"No, I don't want you to come back until your Thanksgiving break. You'll be really busy and it'll be new . . . you'll probably even forget you know me when you meet all those college girls." She pouted and twisted the ring on her finger. Had I been more accustomed to the female subliminal message, I might have realized she was really asking me to leave her alone for a while.

"There won't be any college girls for me. I love you." I waited for her to say she loved me as well. My father waved at us from the field. Some of the other players began pulling into the parking lot. Overhead, thick gray clouds, like flying wool blankets, shrouded the sun. Heavy raindrops clattered like bolts on the roof of my Bel Air. Men scurried like roaches for the dugouts. A toad strangler, one of those quick rising and violent summer thunderstorms common in southern Indiana, blew over us from the west.

"The same."

"What do you mean *the same?* Say you love me too."

"I just want you to be happy."

"Then say the words."

"I don't want to tie you down. Don't you ever think about dating new people? I mean, I can't expect you to be true to me when you're so far away."

"It's only seventy-five miles to Owensboro."

"Yes . . . but . . ."

"Wait a minute. *You* want to see someone else. Who is it?"

"No . . . I just . . ."

"Don't lie to me. Are you already going out on me? You are, aren't you. That's why you don't want to make love because I'll find out you're not a virgin, that you've been giving it away, probably to the whole goddamn baseball team behind my back. Who's getting it tonight, you whore, Bill, maybe John? Who?"

"Sometimes you act completely crazy. You want your ring back? You want to break up? Here, asshole."

Even with the angora, the ring slid off easily and ended up in my lap. We argued for several more minutes, she attempting to get me to end our relationship so she could continue to grow beyond me, while I struggled desperately to hang on to the one public illusion that helped define me and make me unique in the world. I was the guy getting to "third base" with the delectable, blonde cheerleader. Eventually, with more begging than reasoning, I talked her into taking back the ring. We kissed. We petted. After all, with rain pouring down and the windows fogged, no one could see in.

Life seemed to return to its normal ebb and flow when one of the oddest incidents in my life occurred. Unfortunately, I wasn't nearly experienced or wise enough to appreciate the resonance of metaphor. Had I been, it might have prepared me mentally for the pain and humiliation of the next few months.

The sky simply folded into itself and the clouds opened like flower petals. An eerie green glow replaced the gray daylight. The rain stopped and the air quit moving, as if a huge bell jar had been placed over us all and we sat in a vacuum waiting to run out of breath. In an instant, the silence gave way to a loud roar almost like a steam engine locomotive. The clouds returned at great speed and one of them had a tail. The tail whirled in a vortex that I recognized as a twister, but it didn't reach anywhere near ground level. Katie and I watched in amazement, paralyzed by curiosity as much as fear, while it dipped across the ball field and barely touched the top of the tin roof on the grandstand, lifting it away and crumpling it like paper. The twister spit out the roof, now a ball of wrinkled tin, and it fell a few yards behind my back bumper. My ears popped from the air pressure and metal rolled across the parking lot with the sound of an empty beer can.

At first, everyone around the ball park seemed shocked, unable to assess what had just occurred. Then slowly we left our cars and stared at the vacant sky. The men working on the field who had taken shelter in the dugout ran toward us to make sure no one was injured. A couple of cars in the parking lot had been slightly scratched by the rolling roof, but our team escaped unscathed.

My father reached us, his face pale and his eyes glazed over with concern.

"You came very close to being touched by the finger of God," he said. "Don't forget how lucky you were today."

I remembered that storm when I left for college, and the idea that it passed over me when it could have destroyed me buoyed an already overconfident assumption that I was put on the earth for something special. Nothing could harm me till my destiny had been fulfilled, and at that point my destiny seemed to be ending up in the major leagues with a huge salary that my future wife Katie would be overjoyed to spend. I had no knowledge of rhetoric in those days, or I would have known that anytime anyone, including God, tells you something it has both a positive and a negative application. As my father always said, life is like bread. When it gets sliced there are always two sides. Perhaps some god had simply been warning me how easily dreams get smashed and I remained too ignorant to pay attention. After all, I had received a baseball scholarship while playing a game with a broken hand earlier in the season, and even though the hand wasn't completely healed when I resumed play, I managed to keep my batting average above .400. My girlfriend couldn't live without me and the draft board gave me a student deferment to keep me out of Vietnam. Gasoline was twenty-six cents a gallon and Bob Dylan had just released *Highway 61 Revisited*. How much closer to paradise could an eighteen-year-old boy get and still be breathing?

* * *

The fall semester at Kentucky Wesleyan zipped by the way I expected. I made the dean's list with a 3.8 grade-point average and it looked like I might start at second base for the baseball team in the spring. There were signs I could have paid attention to if I hadn't been having so much fun being away from home and actually learning new things. The letters from Katie had almost ceased. I wrote faithfully and waited for return messages of love that never came. When I called on the weekends, she had always gone to the market or a movie with friends and left her mother to tell me she'd call back later. She almost never did. During the four-day Thanksgiving break, we argued about petty things. When we weren't fighting, she remained silent, distant. I remained oblivious, concerned with myself and my budding life.

Then I came home for a three-week Christmas break a day early. I remember it as a typical mid-December day in Princeton, Indiana, a day devoid of color. Gray hung over the frame houses and slid along the curbs and sidewalks of the blocks of streets. The top of the courthouse spun a web of unlit Christmas lights to various street lamps planted in the town square. Dampness seeped under doors and windowsills, not really rain and not really snow, but rather a sort of cold, wet blanket that began to fray only at the edges of fireplaces and space heaters. Still, I felt happy. I was going to see my girlfriend. People lined the sidewalks, shopping, talking, laughing, and living with the stoic sense of resignation that insulates Hoosiers from the drabness and monotony that drives people on both coasts crazy.

I found Katie in a strange man's car doing unspeakable things to him with her tongue. I might have jumped from my own car and dragged him out by the scruff of his neck, thrashing him in the street. I might have, but as I said, the usurper of my love was an auto mechanic I knew who was in his early twenties, not a teenager. My confidence destroyed by Katie's betrayal, I hesitated, unsure I could actually do what I wanted to do to a grown-up. This reaction had no bearing on my personal safety. I wasn't afraid of damaging my own body, or the pain that would follow. My actions in the tunnels and tree lines of Vietnam established that a year later. The probability of embarrassment overrode the rage. If the man turned the tables and beat my ass, not only would he have taken my woman but the rest of my manhood as well. This chance of humiliation seemed more than I could live with at the time, so I snuck away unnoticed to lick my emotional wounds like a dog.

* * *

After my disillusioning Christmas vacation, the second semester at college disintegrated before me. I drank my way through fraternity rush and pledged Sigma Phi Epsilon. Although the pledge hazing prepared me to a limited degree for the dehumanizing demands of Marine Corps boot camp a few months later, it distracted me from my studies and increased the downhill speed and size of the rolling snowball in my brain that my father called "the real world." By April 1967 I had quit attending classes and was failing all but one. The baseball coach dismissed me out of hand before I ever set a spike onto the field, and I didn't even bother complaining. I simply had no interest in anything. Vietnamese poet Nguyen Koa Diem once wrote, "the heart makes an endless day." My days wore on endlessly and I longed for excitement, adventure, to be needed and wanted. Boredom often cultivates stupidity. I found myself reading and believing that America was winning its little war in Southeast Asia and the idea that I might help save my country from the Communist hordes took seed and grew in that bored, stupid area of my mind as another goal to be pursued by my chaotic spirit.

* * *

I had seen my father uncontrollably angry only once before in my life. On February 5, 1964, I passed the test and received my first driver's license. Like any normal boy, I felt ecstatic because driving a car presented me with the opportunity of getting laid. I had yet to meet Katie and was dating no one in particular, but Dad said he would allow me to use a new car on Valentine's Day provided I found a date for the dance. Things often work in tandem. By having a new car available, getting a date was an easy task. Most of the girls, at least the ones I was acquainted with at the tender ages of fifteen or sixteen, lived in a world that equated fancy cars and pockets full of money with worthiness.

I picked a young woman whose reputation for a certain willingness to allow touching in strategic areas preceded her. She accepted my offer and my father, beaming that his son was "a chip off the old block," handed me the keys on the evening of February 14. In my best Neru jacket and black turtleneck, I drove to the Rexall Drug Store and bought a red, heart-shaped box of chocolates with a pink bow.

The girl seemed so excited at getting the candy, I cut the dance short and drove out of town to a deserted cornfield off of Seedtick Road. Overwhelmed by the prospect that lay before me, I took no notice of the temperature. Night had fallen on an unseasonably warm day. The darkness remained above freezing and the ground thawed into a soup of slippery corn husks and topsoil.

My date put her candy box under the passenger-side front seat and we climbed into the back. After an intense hour or so of kissing and fondling her breasts under her sweater, I managed to get her stretched out across the seat. Climbing on top and grinding into her moving pelvis with my clothes on created more friction than my inexperienced libido could bear and I exploded all over the inside of my Fruit of the Loom underwear. Trying to hide the shame of premature ejaculation, I jumped up and made an excuse about having to get the car home before my father grounded me for being late.

We climbed back over the seats, and as the girl straightened her clothing, I started the car. Throwing it into reverse, I intended to back out of the cornfield and onto the gravel road, but all the tires did were spin in the mud. The more they spun, the more I panicked and gunned the engine. It never occurred to me to try and pull forward and rock the car out of the hole the slipping tires created because the way I needed to go was backward. Within a few minutes, the smell of burning rubber filled the air and the car had buried itself in the muck all the way above the back bumper. In a state of near hysteria, I saw my driving privileges revoked by my father, my high school friends deriding my clumsiness, and this girl telling all her friends what a lame lover I was. Before I ever got out of the car, I had become the laughingstock of Princeton High School. My life was ruined.

Finally facing the inevitable, the girl and I hiked back up the gravel to Highway 41 and caught a ride from a passing motorist. These were the pre-Charlie Manson days and people would still pick up stranded kids along the roadways of America. The driver let us out in the town square and I walked my date home. She provided a don't-call-me-I'll-call-you kiss goodnight and I left to find a pay phone at an all-night laundromat on south Main Street.

When my father arrived at the laundromat, awakened by the call, he was less than pleased, but not terribly angry. He understood that accidents sometimes happen, but what he wanted to know was why it happened "where it happened." I should have been at the dance.

I had a father who demanded that my behavior be better than his and a mother who blanched at the mention of anything sexual. I felt ashamed that I had been stupid enough to hang a new car up in the mud and possibly damage it on my first time driving alone at night. That was my father's shame. At the same time, I felt too self-conscious and embarrassed to explain that the incident had come about while I attempted sex with a loose woman. That was my mother's shame. What does a teenage boy do at these ambivalent times? He lies.

"I took my date home early from the dance. It was boring. I wasn't sleepy, so I was just taking a drive out in the country. You know, thinking about things like where I might want to go to college and what to get mom for her birthday next week."

"Thinking? Someone who doesn't do homework if it interferes with *The Twilight Zone* or *Laugh-In?*"

"Yeah. I'm getting to the age where certain things are taking on an importance in my life. Anyway, I'm driving along and this pickup truck with those huge off-the-road wheels comes flying down Seedtick Road straight at me with his headlights off. I had no choice but to swerve out of his way. That's when I ended up in the field. I tried to get a license number. That guy deserves to be arrested."

"Too dark, huh?"

"What color was the truck? You saw that in your headlights, right?"

"Uh . . . uh . . . black. It was black. That's why I didn't notice it earlier."

By the time we finished our conversation, we arrived at the buried car. Dad got out and walked around it in the field. He opened the passenger side door and looked under the seat. Reaching in, he extracted the box of chocolates my date had left on the floorboard when we first parked.

"What kind of an inconsiderate girl would leave her candy?"

"Maybe she didn't like them."

"Oh, I think she did. Now, are you sure that what you said happened is what happened?"

"Yeah."

A look of disappointment clouded my father's face, but it quickly gave way to a rush of red rage, made even more terrifying in the eerie yellow glow of the dome light in his car.

"Don't you find it funny that I would get a call from your little date telling me she forgot her candy when you and her were out here playing tits and ass and asking would I have you get the box of chocolates for her?" His voice trembled and the pitch rose. "I find that strange given the fact she was already home and you were just out here looking at the goddamn stars all by yourself. Right?"

"Oh yeah . . . maybe . . ."

"Maybe . . . what? Maybe you're a goddamn liar."

"I didn't mean . . ."

"I can stand anything in this world but a liar. A liar's worse than anything. You can't trust one and I'm not going to raise one. You ever tell me a lie again and I'll break your fucking jaw."

I believed he meant it. My father had many flaws, but dishonesty wasn't one of them. I never knew what made him so adamant about speaking and acting truthfully. I only knew that he did and would not tolerate the heir to his name to do otherwise. It was what I respected most about him. It also hurt me to disappoint him. We never spoke of the incident again. I received the obligatory punishments—loss of driving privileges for a while, forfeit of my allowance, etc. Those things I could live with much easier than the memory of how close to completely losing control of his temper my father had come.

This was the kind of reaction I expected once again when I told him two years later in May 1967 that I had flunked out of college and, on the way home, enlisted in the Marine Corps, volunteering for a tour of duty in Vietnam.

We had taken a drive, as we often did, when either of us needed to say something to the other that might be unpleasant. For some reason, he parked the car in front of the public library and across the street from the Boys Club. I have no idea why he made that choice, or even if it was a conscious one. I do remember it though because it struck me in hindsight, as things often do, as another one of those symbolic situational metaphors. Our days of father/ child talks had ended and the days of his trying to reason with me as an adult were beginning.

When I told him what I'd done all of the color drained from his normally tanned and swarthy face. I cringed against the pas- senger-side door, irritated like any ordinary young man who gets lectured frequently, and waited for his cheeks to flush and the yell- ing to begin. I'd heard it all before—how I was going to be a fail- ure in life, how I squandered my God-given talent, how selfish and spoiled I was, how I was going to disappoint my mother. It didn't happen. He lit one of his Dutch Masters cigars and fell silent for a long time, blowing smoke and watching it roll over the inside of the windshield. Finally, a hard expression unlike anything I'd ever seen before crowded over his face and clouded his eyes. Like a diamond has facets, fear and anger and confusion all combined to create the shine of sadness.

"You have no idea what you've done," he said, almost in a whisper.

"I think I do. It's time I did something responsible like serve my country."

"There are ways to serve without going to war, especially this one."

"You went. Now it's my turn. I'm going to get drafted anyway. I wanted to choose my future."

"You think you get to choose your future in the military?" He shook his head. "No man makes his future in war. The future doesn't exist."

"I think you're upset because I might win more medals than you."
I squirmed a little and my T-shirt stuck to the back of the vinyl seat.
I thought for sure that by throwing down this challenge, I'd get a rise
from him. His hushed and subdued demeanor was out of character
and confusing for me. I wanted the familiar anger back.

"Listen to me, boy, if you never listen to another thing I say.
The Marine Corps is carrying the brunt of this war on the ground
in Vietnam and a lot of kids your age are dying. War isn't about
medals and there are no heroes. You sometimes get a medal in
the process of trying to survive. For the infantry, war is a matter of
survival. It isn't like the movies. Guns run out of bullets and the
dead stay dead."

"I'm not afraid," I lied.

"That's because you haven't been and don't know, or because
you're insane. In your case, probably both."

The morning sun got very warm through the windshield. A
few old people walked out of the library. Some professional-look-
ing people shuffled by on their way to or from the courthouse. A
pigeon landed on the sidewalk beside the car and began glean-
ing some discarded candy wrappers for leftovers. My father's eyes
moistened at the corners.

"I'll be okay," I said, embarrassed that my father seemed ready
to cry.

"I hope so, for your mother's sake. I don't feel right about this
war. Some of the things I'm reading in the paper and seeing on
the news don't add up to what the politicians are saying. I'm not
sure we're there for the right reasons. But what's done is done.
Keep your head down."

"I will."

"No, I mean now when we go home to tell your mother." He
smiled and I felt us cross a barrier. He had just come to realize

that my life had grown out from under his shadow. He couldn't protect me any longer. While that would create anxiety in him for the next several years because of the way I learned to live on the edge in Vietnam and the way I continued to need that adrenaline rush when I came home, I also sensed some relief in him, as if something gripped tightly inside him for a long time had just been released.

We did go home and tell my mother. She cried for hours and fed me my favorite meals for days before I left. My father took a vow that from the time I landed in Vietnam until I came home safely he would not drink any alcohol, based on the idea that my sacrifice would be shared somehow by him. This was an unbelievably difficult vow for him to make, but he lived up to it. He told me when I left that this particular war was one America shouldn't be fighting, an unusual opinion for a conservative World War II veteran in Indiana. I didn't want to believe him. I needed justification to hold my anxieties in check. By the time I came home from my war, I had learned to respect his insight and he had grown more positive and more vocal in opposition to the war. My father lost some lifelong friends, but he never regretted his stance. It was honest and right in his mind.

In early June 1967, I took a Greyhound bus from the old Vann Hotel bus stop on Main Street in Princeton, Indiana, to Louisville, Kentucky. There, among hundreds of enlistees and draftees, I passed my induction physical and took an oath to protect my country from its enemies, even at the cost of my life. That cost seemed miniscule to me at the time because I was immortal.

Chapter 5

BLIND BARBER

Earl cut my hair for years before I learned he saw nothing beyond his eyelashes. Those prism-thick, wire-rimmed specs magnified the red veins in his eyes for people looking in and not much else. "Quit worrying," he said. "The difference between a good cut and a bad one's only two weeks." And then he felt around my head as if it were a ripe peach, searching for a spot where the fuzz was longest. He called those cuts burrs back in the early 1960s in Princeton, Indiana. But if Earl felt the least bit artistic, he would pull up short of a complete peeling and guide the clippers at perfect level across the top of my head about a half inch from the scalp. This radical design he called a flattop, named after the nickname for aircraft carriers. It made sense because the top of my head resembled a runway and, what with the bobbing and weaving I did trying to be cool when I prowled the hallways of Princeton High School, I appeared as a rudderless ship adrift on the high seas.

The most important aspect of Earl's burrs and flattops lay in the irony of each one. We all wanted to fit in, to look the same back in those early days before the social revolution, thinking as we did that our conformity hid a measure of independence as well as security. The safest way to survive high school came through being in the right collective. Groups like the one I belonged to with my short hair maintained their own pecking order and shielded their members from the pecking that went on at the fringes of our cruel society. I was a "jock" and a popular one, well known for my athletic ability and my overconfident attitude throughout the hallowed halls. Attack me and get attacked by the football team in the fall, the basketball team in the winter, and the baseball team in the spring. We were the boys who made fun of fat girls, clumsy nerds in gym class, freshmen with pimples, and the ugly, the crippled, the crazy.

In other words, I grew up as a privileged asshole, not because my parents taught me the way of arrogance, but rather because I felt the power of being physically fit and well trained and of belonging to a special group marked by the same haircuts. I liked it. Had I paid closer attention to detail, I would have learned the lesson Earl, the blind barber, inadvertently tried to teach me before I enlisted in the Marine Corps and became part of the ultimate clique, the one that would shape my life for years to come. I never received the same haircut twice. It was an illusion. By virtue of his vision trouble, Earl nicked a different spot on my scalp every two weeks and each time created a different portrait of who Jim McGarrah was.

The art of living, as distinguished from just existing, lies in the ability to be different, to grow and change, evolve into something greater than the sum of its parts. When everyone looks and acts the same, the beauty of humanity can often become the beast. A burr haircut begins that descent.

It happened to me almost immediately when I got shoved through the screen door of the little post barbershop on Parris Island, South Carolina, in the spring of 1967. But it was too late and I was too stunned, like a cow in the chute of a slaughterhouse, for philosophic self-awareness. That came years later in an amphetamine-induced frenzy of epiphanies at a Led Zeppelin concert.

I don't want to spend a lot of time reiterating what has already been said about Marine Corps boot camp in many books and films, beginning with Jack Webb in *The D.I.* and running all the way through Stanley Kubrick's *Full Metal Jacket.* The important aspect of boot camp is the erasing of individual thought and replacing

Marine boot camp graduation photo, 1967.

it with an obsession to follow orders, even if it means your death. Something very similar takes place in the thoroughbred horse-racing industry. A good horse trainer builds his charge emotionally (yes, horses have some basic emotions) and physically to the point of exploding, and then channels that chaos and primal instinct through pain, humiliation, and discipline. When the animal has reached peak condition and power, it's unleashed on a racetrack. Does it go crazy? No. The horse runs to the point of destroying itself in a controlled pattern toward a predetermined goal. It does as it's been trained to do without question. How well it's been trained often plays a role in the racehorse's survival.

Something very similar takes place in the Corps, a breaking down physically and emotionally followed by a building up. How successfully the task gets accomplished depends on the expertise and commitment of the three drill instructors assigned to each new platoon. I had three of the best. The shaved head that I walked out of that little Quonset hut on Parris Island with proved to be just the initial phase of turning Jim McGarrah, the big wheel of Princeton High School, into a small cog of the "lean green fighting machine." From that first day forward, the joy of killing became my mantra and God forbid if anyone in my platoon couldn't keep up with the chanting.

The senior drill instructor, Gunnery Sergeant Bishop, held hypnotic sway over the other two. We, as recruits, saw little of him. He passed orders to a staff sergeant named Smith fresh from decorated duty in Vietnam and to a Cajun sergeant named Thibideaux insane with desire to go to Vietnam and kill something. These two junior drill instructors made Gunny Bishop's wishes come true and helped me appreciate the phrase "shit rolls downhill."

We ran miles every morning before sunrise, marched for hours on the parade deck, maneuvered through the manual of arms, memorized standing orders, negotiated the obstacle courses, ate meals at attention, slept with our M-14 rifles, and learned that our existence was predicated on the success of the unit as a whole. The weak were weaned from the herd, sent to motivation platoon, psych ward, or the brig. All the while, Thibideaux cajoled, screamed, beat, kicked, and badgered his way through the ranks hoping to peel away more weakness. All the while, Smith quietly reminded us that he had been to Vietnam and if we didn't learn to kill without restraint, we would be killed without mercy. After a month of this treatment, one kid from Illinois went absent without leave. They found him under our barracks two days later trying to eat a tube of Crest toothpaste—a tube of Crest, complete with fluoride, would kill most humans. The military police dragged him in restraints to the nut farm. One kid from Kentucky stole the Cajun's car and tried to run the main gate. The MP on duty put a bullet in his shoulder.

Thibideaux got reprimanded for leaving his keys in the ignition. He drooled and stomped around enraged for days. The beatings were severe, but we learned to hold each other together as brothers and to never break or run.

Late in my senior year in high school, I had picked up the habit of smoking Lucky Strikes. In those days, we believed cigarettes to be just another joyful aspect of the American dream. When my uncle was dying of lung cancer at Gibson General Hospital, the nurse would light him a cigarette every hour and insert it into his trachea tube so he could enjoy his last few days. Anyway, by the time I finished a year away from home at college where I could smoke without regard to parental restraint, my habit had become an addiction.

At least half of the platoon smoked and the first thing our drill instructors did when we arrived at Parris Island was remove our cigarettes. I thought I'd have a nervous breakdown for the first three days, and then it was as if I'd never smoked at all. Three weeks passed. No desire to smoke remained in my conscious mind. No nicotine surged through my bloodstream.

One morning, Smith entered the barracks after physical training with a pack of Marlboros. We stood at attention as he circled the squad bay and said, "Smokers remove one cigarette." My hand trembled, seemed unattached and uncontrollable as it reached into the pack and extracted a Marlboro. "Smokers form a smoking circle outside, double-time."

About fifteen or twenty of us ran, single file, out onto the grounds in front of our barracks and formed a tight circle. Smith pushed through and placed a small red bucket half full of water in the center. "You may light your cigarette in a military manner." Still standing at attention, I struck a match and inhaled. The acrid smoke felt glorious in my mouth, my throat, and my lungs. I wouldn't have traded that feeling at that moment for a bus ticket home. "You may smoke one cigarette in a military manner." I raised and lowered my right arm at a sharp angle, bending it only at the elbow, to bring the Marlboro to my lips and take it away. My back straight, my heels together, my head held high, I sucked the life from that tiny tube of tobacco until the burning filter choked me. Everyone else did the same. "Field strip those cigarettes and place the filters in the bucket. If I see one piece of paper on the ground, you WILL run ten miles."

From this point forward, the drill instructors allowed us cigarettes three times a day, but only under their control and only together as a unit. Any individuality I might have felt, delusion or not, by smoking in high school and college, had been stripped away like the cigarette butts. Even my desire to smoke had been removed from me and returned to me by my handlers. This small, intimate, and personal activity was no longer under my control. The body and the mind learned to do only what it was told to do and in harmony with my fellow marines.

*   *   *

Six weeks into training, the platoon turned a corner. I don't know how the rest of the guys made it, but what saved me was the image of another young man from Princeton, Indiana. Ralph had been three years ahead of me in school and had the well-earned reputation of being a fuck-up. He had no discipline, no ambition, very little athletic ability or natural intelligence. Yet he had completed Marine Corps basic training and served with distinction and honor in Vietnam. I constantly held his face in my mind and told myself that I could do anything Ralph could, only better. Fortunately for me, I didn't find out until I went home on leave after my training that Ralph, unable to live with himself after his tour of duty in the war, had wrapped his car around a tree one morning while I ran the obstacle course at Parris Island.

When I say we turned the corner, I mean we evolved into a cohesive unit, taking all awards available at the time, including tactics, marksmanship, and hand-to-hand combat. The brightly colored rainbow of pennants flew proudly from our platoon flagstaff.

Although all of the "non-hackers" who were unfit for the Corps in general had been driven from our unit, there were still a few recruits with specific weaknesses, certain elements of training that they just couldn't seem to master. Since the crazy Cajun's opportunity for promotion and dream trip to combat would be greatly enhanced if the platoon won *every* ribbon and was designated regimental honors platoon, he made these few recruits his special project and tortured them into overcoming their flaws.

As basic training drew to a close, one of the last awards for us was the drill competition. A quiet giant of a man from Mississippi simply couldn't march. As if he had two left feet, he stumbled and whirled in every direction but the right one. Both drill instructors were beside themselves with rage because the man was black. They had no way of understanding how or why a black man lacked *rhythm,* so they took for granted he was lazy and shiftless. Thibideaux referred to him as Mr. Bojangles and took him on private forced marches and through extra drill sessions. Nothing worked.

The night before drill competition, the Cajun came into the barracks alone and stood in the center of the highly waxed wood floor. We sat in our skivvies enjoying thirty minutes of free time before lights out—writing letters, cleaning weapons, or talking about the sex we hoped to have on leave. Thibideaux put his hands on his hips and I could smell the tension seep into the room like sweat and dirt in the locker room during halftime of a football game you're losing badly. We waited as he glared at all of us in turn.

"Bojangles, front and center."

"Sir, yes sir," said Bojangles, the white underwear a stark contrast against his dark skin as he thumped barefooted at a run from the end of his bunk to the tip of Thibideaux's spit-shined boots, where he pulled up short and stood at stiff attention, a mountain of muscle towering over the drill instructor.

"It is inconceivable to me that you are such a fucked-up, clumsy piece of shit disgrace to your race. If your momma knew how clumsy you were, she would have let the Klan burn you instead of a cross in her front yard. No use wasting the wood. Do we all agree that Bojangles is the most fucked-up private in the Marine Corps."

Thibideaux did a slow three-hundred-and-sixty-degree turn, watched us closely, and measured our enthusiasm as we all screamed, "Sir, yes sir!" Facing Private Bojangles again, he started to drool. This drooling was a recurrent problem when he got excited and had earned him, behind his back of course, the nickname Spastic, which we all pronounced "Spaz dick" in moments of extreme bravery.

"The platoon agrees with me, Bojangles. Do you?"

"Sir, yes sir. I'm a clumsy asshole, sir."

"You want to help us win this drill award, right?"

"Sir, yes sir."

"Then go get me your bayonet." Bojangles retrieved it from his footlocker.

The barracks, already silent except for the drooling screech of Spastic's voice, transcended the quiet and entered a vacuum of fear. Even my own breathing became inaudible. No movement, not so much as a breeze through the screened windows, broke the terrible curtain of uncertainty that shrouded the room. I don't know what the other recruits thought, but given Spastic's penchant for unpredictability, I believed anything might be possible. He took the bayonet and ran his fingers over the edges, outlining the foot-long stiletto blade like a blind artist might gauge a great sculpture.

"This weapon is made for killing. Not only that, it's made for killing up close so you get the pleasure of looking in your enemy's eyes as he dies. That's the reward God gives us for keeping heaven populated with fresh souls. Do you believe I could kill you with this right now, Bojangles?" Even Spastic didn't know the answer to that since he'd never really killed anyone before, but we were trained to answer only one way.

"Sir, yes sir," screamed Bojangles.

"The only thing stopping me is the fact that I would have to write a letter to your momma and make her cry. You don't want your momma to cry, do you?"

"Sir, no sir."

"Then I'm not going to kill you. I'm going to ask God to forgive me because I'm going to use this beautiful instrument of death for an unholy purpose. Do you know what that is?"

"Sir, no sir."

"This bayonet is going to teach you how to dance. If you can dance, you can surely march."

"Sir, yes sir."

One of the six other black recruits in our platoon, Private Snowball, made the mistake of squirting out a very small giggle. Thibideaux whirled around and rushed past me and several rigid bodies to Snowball's bunk. Without saying a word, he smacked him open-handed across the side of his head and knocked him down. As soon as Thibideaux saw that the young man remained conscious and started to stand again, he returned to Bojangles.

"Time to dance." Sergeant Spastic Thibideaux, drooling profusely now like a mad dog, flung the bayonet into the floor, intending his charge to hop out of the way, like the old gunslingers in the Wild West made people dance with bullets. Unfortunately, Bojangles was not lazy. His mind just worked a little slower than most minds and he had no idea what game Spastic played. The bayonet did stick in the wood floor, but only after it passed through the private's foot. I know this was not what Spastic intended because his tanned face turned instantly to chalk. His knees buckled slightly, almost imperceptibly. But I swear they did buckle. He must have seen his entire military career disappearing in a haze of court martials, brig time, and disgrace.

A moan began somewhere in the stabbed recruit's lower abdomen, gathering size and momentum as it rose to his lips, like a snowball that has defied gravity rolls uphill, until it burst into the silent air as a wet and terrible squeal, "Feeeeuuuckkk." To his credit and to the credit of our drill instructors for teaching us survival discipline, Bojangles remained at attention. There's no telling how much damage would have occurred had he torn his foot away from the floor.

After what seemed like hours but was in fact only seconds, Spastic regained his composure. He called two of the tallest recruits to Bojangles. They supported him, one beneath each shoulder, as the drill instructor quickly and evenly withdrew the blade and applied direct pressure to the wound with his handkerchief.

"Private McGarrah."

"Sir, yes sir."

"Get a mop from the head and scrub the blood off this floor. Double-time, maggot. If I see a speck of blood on this floor when I get back, I WILL beat your ass severely." I ran as fast as I could to retrieve the mop. By the time I returned to the squad bay area with mop and bucket, Spastic was gone. Bojangles had been loaded in the car and Thibideaux was driving him to the base infirmary. One of the recruits who had helped carry the wounded private told me that our orders were to remain quiet and under no circumstances discuss among ourselves the incident that had just occurred.

Normally, it would have been impossible for a group of young men not to chatter and speculate about an incident like this. But we were not in a normal situation and thought that disobeying an order could generate another response from Spastic like the one we had just seen. The idea of a bayonet piercing various appendages on the body was unpleasant enough to keep us silent and steady.

Sergeant Thibideaux returned alone in an hour.

"Private Bojangles will live. The question is, will all of you? Here's what's going to happen. Private Bojangles reported this incident to the doctor as an accident. He dropped the bayonet on his own foot while cleaning it. Tomorrow, a CIS investigator will enter our world. He may ask several of you what happened. What did happen?"

In unison, the platoon replied, "Sir, Private Bojangles dropped his bayonet on his own foot."

"That's the correct answer and the only answer. If any of you ruin my career by saying something different, I swear to God I'll take that cowardly scumbag to the rifle range and shoot him myself, then make it look like a firing line accident. IS THAT CLEAR?"

"Sir, yes sir." The squad bay echoed in the affirmative. I was pretty sure in my rational mind that the drill instructor hadn't meant what he'd said, but after so many weeks of learning to obey orders, of bonding with the platoon, of thinking only in terms of loyalty and teamwork, and the ever-present fear that Spastic might actually have gone completely crazy, my emotions ran amuck with images of my bloody body lying in a ditch behind the rifle range. I told the Criminal Investigation Services captain the next day exactly what I was supposed to, and I won't pretend I felt guilty about lying instead of good about surviving.

I heard some scuttlebutt a few months later that Spastic Thibideaux got his wish and went to Vietnam, where he was seriously wounded. Shortly after that, Sergeant Smith decided that drill instructing was for pussies and volunteered for a second tour in country. I don't know for sure if either of them lived or died. I *do* know that for all the bluster, the pain, the bullshit, the humiliation and degradation those men put me through, I came out on the other side of boot camp with the physical and emotional tools and the discipline to survive the most horrific, mind-altering, surreal experience I could ever imagine. For that, I thank them.

*   *   *

I never saw Bojangles again. My platoon won drill competition and took regimental honors at graduation. We received our orders. Most of us, myself included, got designated MOS-0311, or infantry rifleman, and were instructed to report for the first leg of our journey to 'Nam—Advanced Infantry Training at Camp LaJeune in North Carolina. After a two-week boot leave, which I spent drunk and trying unsuccessfully to get laid in Princeton, Indiana, I went to North Carolina for a month, and then flew to Camp Pendleton in California for additional training in counterinsurgency and escape and evasion tactics. In September 1967 I walked up the steps into a Continental Airlines jet for the flight to Okinawa, a staging area for replacements of the dead and wounded in Vietnam. Okinawa was a short time and a long way from Kentucky Wesleyan College and the baseball diamonds of the Midwest.

Chapter 6

A MATTER OF PRIORITIES

When I was home on leave from boot camp a few weeks before I went to war, my uncle gave me an expensive wristwatch, the kind with a luminescent face and depth gauge if I ever went scuba diving in the dark. Never mind that the dark and the ocean terrified me.

"You'll always know what time it is with this baby, and it's shock resistant for the explosions."

My uncle had a way of overstating the obvious, especially if it was something you were trying not to think about. But, the watch was beautiful. I'd never seen one like it and I wore it when I flew from home back to the staging area at Camp Pendleton after my boot leave was over. I showed it to the stewardess on the jet that carried me to Okinawa. She smiled at me and with sad eyes said, "I wish it made you bulletproof. You seem like a nice boy." When my unit deplaned and was driven in an old school bus repainted olive drab to Camp Hansen, I passed it back and forth between the marines across the aisle and the driver. I showed it to the gunnery sergeant waiting at the barracks.

"What the fuck's wrong with you, marine? Are you crazy?" he said. "I don't give a good goddamn about that pussy little watch. Hell, one of your bunkmates will probably steal it off your dead body in a few weeks anyway."

As I unpacked the few things I needed from my duffel bag, I tucked the sergeant's words away in my mind so they wouldn't distract me from my new surroundings. I had spent enough time on the flight over thinking about my own death, and this new country smelled, looked, tasted, and sounded different than anything I'd ever imagined in my isolated midwestern life.

We marched in formation to the mess hall for evening chow. It was the usual fare, high in starch and protein, some kind of roasted pseudo-beef with huge globs of mashed potatoes drowned in a dark brown gelatinous substance labeled gravy by the mess cooks. I ate more from force of habit than hunger while I listened to the other marines at my table talk about how they had saved most of last month's pay so they could go into the village outside Camp Hansen, get drunk, and buy some whores. Buy some whores— another experience that had totally slipped by me in small-town pubescent training. Actual pay-as-you-go women seemed always to be in short supply in southwestern Indiana, although we had one old man with false teeth who hung out at the pool room and would pay good money to sneak into the restroom and watch us piss, extra if you let him hold your dick. I guess that made us sort of pay-as-you-go boys.

Thank God the next day was payday because I'd spent every dime available at home on leave, and I desperately wanted to try this new thing of purchasing sex before I got killed in Vietnam. This thought dominated all my other thoughts as I checked the time on my scuba-diving, glow-in-the-dark wristwatch. It was 1800 hours by Marine Corps standards and we were scheduled back in formation outside the mess hall. All I knew as we assembled were two things. First, the grizzled old gunnery sergeant who had met us when we arrived was going to march us across the base to a large Quonset hut where we would somehow be oriented to the Orient by way of films and lectures, and second, this first day was passing very slowly on Okinawa now that I had learned that love could be purchased at night for a reasonable fee just outside the main gate of Camp Hansen.

*   *   *

The air in the Quonset hut reeked of sweat tangled in Mennen Skin Bracer and unwashed skivvies. A slight curtain of anxiety seemed to hang over the sea of green bodies filling the straight-backed metal chairs packed tightly in the hut. The hint of fear coupled with the tropical heat and humidity spotted most of the green fatigues with dark blotches of dampness. At 1830 exactly, a strange little man in black-rimmed glasses and tropical dress uniform wearing captain's bars walked to the front, mounting a slightly raised platform. The gunny screamed, "Uh-ten-hut." Chairs rattled, boot heels clacked, men stood, and backs went straight.

"At ease men." We sat back down. "Can everyone hear me?"

"Aye aye sir." I chanted in unison with my fellow warriors turned students.

"I'm the liaison officer on this base and it's my job to educate you to the perils of Vietnam. You know that, as marines, you are expected to die by the sword. I'm here to tell you that there are far more insidious and horrible ways to die that may take you unawares. Military intelligence has brought to our attention that some Russian Commie scientists have introduced an incurable strain of gonorrhea into South Vietnam. Many of the whores there are infected with this black clap and the disease is so powerful that it eats through condoms."

The room filled with loud sighs. Some of the men shook their heads, and the private sitting on my right whispered, "Leave it to the fucking gooks."

"Let me continue. If you are infected with this black clap, you will be shipped back here to Okinawa and transferred to a small island just off of this coast where you will wait in the hospital there and eventually die an excruciatingly painful death. Your parents will be notified that you are missing in action and presumed dead.

The Marine Corps cannot risk allowing you to return home and spread this disease to innocent civilian American women."

Again, a loud collective sigh filled the air, and marines began to squirm, faces contorted, and the private on my right whispered, "Leave it to the fucking gooks."

"Calm down men. There is no way you can catch this disease unless you screw Vietnamese whores. Keep it in your pants and do your job, which is to kill the enemy and not fuck them. Let me reinforce what I've told you by reminding you that many of these gook whores are also VC, have relatives in the VC, or are married to VC soldiers. If you don't heed my warning, you may be lucky enough to avoid the black clap but find yourself screwing a VC sympathizer who is using a Gillette razor blade as her diaphragm. In this scenario you will remove only the bloody stump of your dick."

At this point in the lecture, the liaison officer had a corporal in the rear of the hut dim the lights and turn on a film projector.

"What you are about to witness is a group of men in the last stages of black clap."

The film was a grainy, low budget, black-and-white Department of Defense production and the sound track crackled and popped so loudly that the dialogue was inaudible. Vacuum-eyed men in hospital gowns lay in a ward that could have been in any building at any time anywhere on the planet. The camera panned over the room, zooming in at strategic intervals to give us a close-up of moaning patients covered with leprous-looking scabs, and then settled on an army officer behind a desk. Staring straight into our eyes, the officer spoke rapidly in clipped, guttural language. I could make out about every third word. "These . . . goodtime . . . sex . . . death . . . families . . . duty . . . lust . . . the . . . ." The film ran off one reel and the loose end rattled against the wrapped celluloid on the other. The screen went black.

"Lights, corporal," said the captain. "Are there any questions?"

It was seven o'clock, almost one minute after seven, when the questions began. No, it was one minute after. No, it was one minute and three seconds after. No, it was . . . .

"Has anyone ever lived through the black clap?"

"Never."

"What if we go on R&R to Thailand? Do the whores there have it?"

"To my knowledge, only our enemies have it."

"What happens if you wear two condoms?"

"A good question. Ask a navy corpsman for the answer."

"Do gook whores have slanted pussies, sir?"

"Marine, that's absurd. Unlike the truthful statements you just heard from me, that's a myth concocted by the enemy to make you curious. Don't believe it."

"How much do they cost?"

"What?"

"The whores, sir. How much do they cost?"

At this point in the presentation, the captain removed his black-rimmed eyeglasses and wiped the sweat from his flooding brow with a handkerchief he had pulled from his back pocket. The peanut-butter color of his tropical dress uniform was darkening beneath the arms and under his breasts from sweat. He seemed resigned to the fact that all his hard work had fallen on deaf ears.

"I have no idea how much these women charge, private. But your question does remind me of another subject that we need to cover regarding your brief stay here at Camp Hansen, pay and off-base privileges."

Since our normally scheduled payday was less than twenty-four hours away and since the Okinawan neon night began a few feet from the back gate and since we were going to be here for two nights before flying into Da Nang, I waited anxiously for the captain to explain when our pay would be delivered and how soon after that we could give it away to the fine females of this fair island.

"It has been our experience in the past that young marines with their pockets full of money sometimes briefly forget their primary mission. In the past, we've temporarily lost good men to the pleasures of Okinawa. It has been an unnecessary waste of military time and money rounding up hungover marines just to get them on the plane out of here, not to mention the broken bar glass and various other property damages and ill will created among the citizens of this island. For God's sake men, this is somebody's home!"

The captain began pacing the platform and flapping his arms as if he might take off into the rafters of the Quonset hut like a trapped and frightened starling. I, on the other hand, being a fairly good student of history during my brief stay at a small midwestern college, sat still and remembered quite clearly that this certainly was somebody's home. Just twenty-two years before, several thousand Japanese soldiers dug into the caves around this island with one purpose—to kill as many marines as possible. The fighting on Okinawa at the close of World War II had been some of the most brutal and costly of the whole campaign. Now, of course, our government needed the strategically placed speck of land as a hub for troops and equipment to control Southeast Asia, so suddenly "this was somebody's home, for God's sake." The political bullshit bored me. I was checking my watch again when the captain's next statement almost ruined my life.

"Therefore, in the best interest of you men personally, the Marine Corps, and the fine citizens of this country, it has become standard operating procedure to suspend pay and off-base privileges to all transient personnel. You will not draw your pay until you arrive in Vietnam."

The private next to me whispered under his breath again, "Leave it to the fucking gooks," and the room hummed like a nest of angry bees.

"Don't forget there's a free movie in this hut beginning at twenty hundred hours. It's one of my personal favorites, *The Sands of Iwo Jima*, starring our favorite American John Wayne."

The gunnery sergeant called us all to attention and we stood in bitter silence as the captain left the stage. "Dismissed."

I walked back to the barracks alone and wrote a letter to my parents telling them not to worry. I was having the time of my life. Then I slept the sleep of the dead.

*   *   *

After breakfast at the mess hall the next morning, I walked over to the post exchange. I had no money but a lot of time, as my wristwatch kept reminding me on its slow journey from second to minute and minute to hour. The more I looked at it, the slower the hands moved. Now that my chance to get laid seemed to have disappeared, I wanted to involve myself in the only other reason a young man lives, the illusion of war. The sooner this day passed and I boarded the C-130 aircraft for Da Nang the next morning, the better. It had become time to get on with the killing.

The PX was an overwhelming mixture of shiny objects and the smell of disinfectant. Cameras, radios, canned goods, washing machines, televisions, and coffeepots either lined rows and rows of shelves or were stacked on the waxed tile floor. Without taxes, the prices on everything were as good as could be found on the back of a black-market truck in most American inner cities. Obviously, the goods in the store catered to career personnel living on base, not grunts on the way to war. Anyway, I had exactly twenty-six cents in my pocket and everything I needed stowed away in my duffel bag back at the barracks. I did buy one pack of Pall Mall cigarettes for eleven cents.

"Mighty nice looking watch," said a voice behind me at the cash register. I turned and met a tall lance corporal who wore a black military police patch on his right shoulder. He had a disarming smile and an easy sort of manner that made him seem familiar and interested in my response.

"My uncle gave this to me when I left the States."

"Want to sell it?"

"Why? I can't do anything with the money. We're restricted to base till we leave tomorrow and there's nothing I need here."

"That base restriction thing might not be as serious as it sounds."

Curious, I followed the MP as he motioned for me and we walked out behind the PX. Staying about ten feet away from the perimeter fence, we circled the camp until arriving at a guard shack at one of the back gates used to bring in supplies. Another MP inside the shack waved and the lance corporal gave him a thumbs-up.

"Don't be too obvious, but look about ten meters to the right of the gate, behind and out of sight of the guard's post."

I could see a small section of chain-link fence where the bottom didn't quite reach into the ground, as if a small dog had dug its way out in search of a bone.

"I've got the night detail at this post. That hole is big enough for a man to wiggle through and disappear into the streets. All you got to do is make sure you come back in before I get off duty."

"Why tell me this?"

"Commerce, my man, commerce. You got a nice watch. I give you ten bucks and look the other way. You give me the watch, go into the village, and get some pussy to write home about before you get killed in country. I get the watch before it gets broken and sell it at a later date. Think of it as your own personal wake thrown by you. You might as well party now because you won't have time to party where you're going, which is another reason why you don't need the watch. No one wants to know how much time he's got left in country. It's bad luck. So, what about it? It's a matter of priorities."

The lance corporal's logic made perfect sense to me, and there in the blinding white sun, standing on the blinding white sand, I unbuckled my uncle's present, trading it quickly for a ten-dollar bill. I even felt relief. Not to be burdened by the measuring of my steady progress from birth to death brought about a lightness of being. I won't say I felt no guilt. My uncle paid almost a hundred dollars for that wristwatch, which in 1967 was a week's pay for him. As absolution for my sin of lust, I left the lance corporal, returned to the barracks, and spent the afternoon writing a long letter to my uncle about how the watch had saved my life in my very first firefight, but had been smashed in the process. I lied eloquently and then tucked the letter safely away so I could mail it when I got to Vietnam the next morning. All I had to do was stay alive for fifteen minutes after the plane landed and find the post office.

* * *

A good marine rifleman is as much at home in the dark as in the light. At 1900 hours, I slipped away from the barracks. Turning down several requests from fellow marines I passed to attend the free movie with them, I made lame excuses about needing time alone to meditate and pray about our mission in Vietnam, or think about my girlfriend Katie who had left me for an older man that worked as a car mechanic back home, or check my equipment, or do some extra physical training to work off stress. Then, I found the hole in the fence and scurried under it, crab-like, into the humid arms of the Asian night.

Strolling through the backstreet shadows just off base, I veered around the first corner and walked into a carnival. The narrow streets rolled up and down with waves of small brown people. American servicemen in garish, rainbow-colored Hawaiian shirts occasionally parted the Asian masses like giant white stones in the middle of a river. I tried to stay away from the Americans because I didn't want to run into any shore patrol or military police and be asked to produce an off-base pass that I didn't have.

The air crackled thick and electric. The energy of rock-and-roll music blasting from the dozens of barrooms and the hawking sounds from the sidewalk vendors almost made me afraid to touch anything, like I had walked across a long carpet and would get shocked if I tried to open the door. All around me was another reason I enlisted in the military, not the reasons I told myself six months earlier, not to kill or be killed like a rabid dog, not out of some sense of patriotic duty or conscience, not to please the Republicans in my hometown, but rather to taste, hear, see, touch, and feel a new world, a world so unlike my own that I could some-how become greater than the sum of my midwestern American parts. I had grown hungry.

No, really, I had grown hungry. The smells of roasted duck, barbecued pork, soy, and the strange spices that I learned only later were ginger, cumin, curry, and thyme seeping from the open doorway on my immediate right reminded my body that it had missed mess call at 1800 hours. Most people here for the first time would have called the smells exotic. To me, they were erotic. As I turned toward the brightly lit café, a Japanese man in a white shirt and black slacks grabbed my elbow and gently urged me forward through the door.

"You eat Okinawa style. Enjoy my hometown and we talk." I must have looked skeptical because he quickly added, "No, no, we talk for free. You keep your money for dessert later. I show you." Winking and chuckling, he steered me toward a rickety bamboo table just big enough for the two of us and bowed. "I am Mr. Chiba. You are?"

"Call me Jim."

"Okay. Ichariba choodee."

"What's that mean?"

"Here, it means once we meet and talk, we are brothers."

Still slightly bowed, he backed away from the table, listed left, dodged a couple leaving, and began talking to a man in a white apron behind the counter. I hadn't seen any MPs on the street and felt pretty secure. I guess I should have been more anxious being alone in this place, but a strange sense of well-being overwhelmed me. I thought of my father's words when I was a small child and went to the dentist, "Think of the worst thing that could happen to you in this situation and then know that it won't." The worst thing I could think of was finding out the food here tasted like cheeseburgers and fries. The huge bottle of "33" beer Mr. Chiba brought me as he sat back down and the poster of Jimi Hendrix I saw hanging from the wall eased my slight misgivings even more, especially the words scrawled in English beneath the poster, "Jimi is to the guitar what God is to the wind."

Following closely on my host's tail trudged the cook with a tray of steaming white bowls. Various colorful and fragrant dishes sat before me.

"You start with egg flower soup. Very delicious," said Mr. Chiba. "Ground pork, shiitake mushrooms, mustard cabbage, soup stock. Very good for you."

He was right. How could anything that tasted so wonderful and new be anything but the magic elixir of long life? The people on this island were known the world over for their longevity. I ate the soup quickly and started on something called *rafute*, which Mr. Chiba told me contained pork as well, but also bonito stock, soy sauce, rice wine, and my new favorite spice, ginger. Finishing the meal with a cinnamon and sugar *nantu*, I rubbed my belly and reached in my pocket to pay the bill with part of the precious ten dollars I earned by selling my watch.

"No pay. My gift. Now, I take you for dessert and there I get paid commission by old lady who run the place. You pay her with American money and I leave to find a new friend. She take good care of you. No diseases."

"Oh man, you must mean sex. Shit, I don't know if I've got enough time. I've got to be back on base before the guard shift changes."

"What time does guard change?"

I brought my wrist up to eye level automatically. It was bare.

"I forgot to ask. I don't even know what time it is now."

"You don't know because time only important if you in prison," said Mr. Chiba. That seemed like a very good point.

*   *   *

My guide hustled me through a maze of flashing neon lights. The air covered us both like a wet wool blanket, but only I seemed bothered by the humidity and heat. Mr. Chiba was a man directed by a higher calling, his commission, and as such paid no heed to the world outside his own mind. I knew this because he kept mumbling, "Hurry up. I got to find at least two more customers, or I go home poor again." We crisscrossed several narrow streets and alleys and, within a few minutes, turned onto a wider boulevard lined with more bars and clapboard hotels. Even though I ran ten miles a day and could easily do several hundred pushups and situps, it was almost impossible to keep to Mr. Chiba's pace, and when we stopped, I panted like a big dog back home in August.

"You stay alive, you better get in shape."

"I don't know what my problem is tonight."

"Never mind. Soon, you feel much better."

I stood in front of a one-story building and watched a blue neon sign above the door as it crackled and spat "Happy Hotel" at me in perfect time with my own heartbeat. The idea that any hotel could be called the Happy Hotel caused me to burst out laughing, as if I'd just seen a parody of this whole evening on Rowan and Martin's television show *Laugh-In*. I half expected Goldie Hawn to stick her head out a window on the nonexistent second story. I felt light-headed, flooded with adrenaline. Everything was hilarious and so visually clear. I seemed to be in and watching a movie at the same time.

Mr. Chiba went inside and, through the plate-glass window, I saw him animatedly conferring with an older Japanese woman. Her black and silver hair was pulled back into a bun so tight it stretched her eyes upward and outward, making them slant into narrow slits like a snake. Had I been in Vietnam at the time, I could have been convinced easily that she was my enemy.

Mr. Chiba threw up his hands and shook his head in disgust. He came out of the hotel shoving a couple of bills in his pocket.

"Mama-san one tough bird, like scrawny old chicken ready for cooking pot. Maybe I wring her neck. You okay. Number one deal for you. I fix everything. You follow her."

The only person I knew in this strange place stuck out his hand to shake mine. "I go now. Back to work." For the first time since I had snuck off the base, I felt queasy and uncertain, second guessing myself. Not that second guessing was unusual for me. I had always been a slave to impulse. My father always told me "a fool learns by experience, a wise man by what he's told." I never bothered remembering those words until I found myself questioning my spontaneity after the fact with my better judgment, and then it was usually too late. That's how I broke my leg stealing home in the baseball tournament, how I got expelled from school for going swimming at the strip pits instead of sitting in algebra class, how I lost my scholarship to college by attending too many keg parties, and how I ended up joining the Marine Corps. Everything I did on a whim came back to bite me in the ass. Now, I was getting stranded illegally off base in a foreign country. My uncle's watch was gone for one tenth of its worth. I had to get back through a hole in a fence before the guard changed and I didn't even know in what direction to start walking.

"Mr. Chiba, you can't leave. What am I supposed to do? How do I get back to the base? I've only got ten dollars and I don't know where I'm at."

"You on Okinawa. You got ten dollars, you rich man. I make deal for you already. Give me one dollar, give mama-san eight dollar." He held up eight fingers and then closed both fists. "You keep one dollar for taxi." Mr. Chiba pointed to the old lady who now stood in the doorway motioning for me to come with her. "She get one for you when you finish good time." My guide extended his right hand, shook mine warmly, and disappeared into a crowd of sailors walking by without looking back.

The old madam walked in front of me, stooped over, but with an air of regal authority at the same time. We passed through a hallway and she opened a door on the right. The room contained a stool, buckets, towels, a massage table, and small hot tub in the center. A thin girl with a pock-marked face, who looked to be in her late teens and wore only a towel, motioned for me to strip. I blushed and hesitated. She motioned again, more urgently. I wasn't a virgin, but I was young and from a small town in southern Indiana. I had gotten what little sexual experience I had in the back seat of various cars on dark country roads from girls who were like me, partly clothed and extremely nervous. To make myself completely vulnerable, especially in front of a disinterested stranger, felt like climbing a mountain with a broken arm.

The walls in the room breathed in and out, expanding and contracting in time with my heartbeat. Steam rose from the hot tub and the thick, wet air burned my lungs. I turned my back to the girl and began removing my clothes. She took them from me, folded them neatly and set them on the floor. Grabbing my hand, she steered my naked body to the stool, where I sat while she wet me down with a sponge, soaped me all over, and then rinsed me with warm water from the bucket. I got the beginning of a hard-on when the girl soaped my balls. Her giggle quickly eliminated it.

Like moving through a car wash, once I was rinsed, I was put into the hot tub. The girl left the room for a few minutes and returned with some fresh towels. She motioned for me to stand and step out of the tub to be dried. I kept waiting for her to have sex with me, but there were no indications that was about to happen. Had Mr. Chiba ripped me off? I lay face down on the massage table and gave myself over to her hands. Suddenly, she jumped on my back and began walking up and down, kneading her toes into my muscles. I felt them go slack beneath her touch and, most amazingly, her whole body seemed to weigh no more than her hands. If Jesus's step had been this light, he certainly would have had no trouble walking on water. Maybe during his missing years, he had spent some time on Okinawa.

Almost in a daze and limp all over, I allowed my masseuse to pull me off the table and fasten a towel around my waist. She piled my clothes in my arms and led me across the hallway to another door. This door opened and a crew-cut American about my age stepped out.

"Don't blink or you'll miss it all," he said, disappearing down the shadowed hallway.

I entered a dim blue haze, so dim I could barely see. If only I had the watch, I would at least know the time. Slowly, my eyes adjusted to the aqua lighting and a small bed rose out of the shadows. I could make out the form of a naked woman lying on the bed, but nothing distinctive about her. Was she pretty? Was she pretty ugly? Did she have scars? It seemed reasonable to assume she was clean because so much effort had been put into cleaning me. Cleanliness had to be something these people on Okinawa prized. I walked toward her. When I stopped in front of her, she jerked my towel away and began mechanically rubbing me with one hand until I was fully erect. The woman hadn't sat up or moved anything but her hand.

I felt like I might burst before I even climbed on and tried everything I could think of to slow down an embarrassing release of semen all over her breasts. I thought about the time I played a football game with a broken thumb; tried to remember my grandmother's birthday, the name of my dog at home, what brand of toilet paper my mother bought; did multiplication tables; and subtracted the number of states starting with "A" from the total number of states. Just when I felt my control going completely, she stopped, and reached under her pillow, extracting an already unwrapped condom and slipping it over my penis as easily as a monkey might peel a banana.

"You get on now. Hurry."

Clumsily, I straddled this person who had never appeared any more defined in my mind than a lump of flesh. She took hold of me and guided me into her.

"Tell me name of girlfriend at home. I whisper to you. Make you happy."

I was on my third or fourth stroke, trying desperately to stutter out a weak "K . . . K . . . K . . . Katie" that I had always wanted, but never had in reality, to make love to. The dam broke and what felt like gallons of liquid shot from the deepest recesses of my being into the reservoir of the condom. I shuddered all over. The woman, who had yet to move, sensed my finale.

"You get off now. More customers waiting."

Before I had time to feel anything that resembled an emotion, I was dressed and out the door, passing a new customer from across the hall.

*   *   *

The old madam waited for me at the end of the hall. She held a glass. Two ice cubes and a maraschino cherry floated in a darker red, fizzing liquid.

"Singapore Sling. Good drink after boom-boom. Part of package deal. Now, you wait while I get taxi."

Sitting on the bamboo stool and sipping the cotton candy–tasting alcohol, I watched the woman shuffle bent backed out the door and wondered if she had been the lump of flesh lying on the bed in the backroom many years ago when these American bases were first built. With time on my hands and no wristwatch to see it pass, I began thinking about the young woman I had just left. A vague sadness filtered into my thoughts. I'm sure now as I look back on this incident that part of the sadness could be qualified as good ol' Christian guilt, the postcoital doubt that church-going farm boys get every time they realize that an orgasm feels great whether you're married or not. I was raised to believe that anything this pleasurable would eventually cause me untold misery and I would deserve whatever happened to me. I had felt this way before with my finger in Katie. But, in the back of my 1957 yellow Chevy Bel Air, I had been able to balance the sadness by lying to myself that I loved the blonde creature with porcelain skin and blue eyes that I petted beneath me, that I would one day marry her and thus pay the dues for my sins.

Trying hard to focus on anything memorable about this Japanese hooker, I found that the dim lighting coupled with my own anxiety had left me able only to recall the vacant, glazed-over black eyes and the lifeless, almost cold, body. I didn't know it then because I was years away from becoming the least bit self aware, but this girl had been teaching me a lesson that saved my sanity during the next few months of horrific violence in the jungles of Southeast Asia. She established her priority, which was the survival of her body in an impoverished and decimated land. She did it by numbing her emotions to the point that she felt no love, no compassion, no joy, no fear, no doubt, no pain, and no hope during the act of sex. Becoming a vessel for the deposits of countless men was a job nothing more, as killing would become for me.

The taxi pulled up. I walked out onto the street and jumped in the backseat while the old lady held the door and bowed.

"I want to go to Camp Hansen but not the front gate. When we get there, I'll have to try and remember which gate I left from."

"No problem," said the driver. "You go to gate with hole in fence like other marines who got no pass. Lance Corporal Mike fix you up?"

"He was a lance corporal, but I didn't catch his name."

"What it cost you?"

"A wristwatch."

"What?"

"A wristwatch," I said again and leaned across the seat to tap my vacant wrist.

"Corporal Mikey one smart marine. Maybe you not so smart."

The beat-up little taxi hurtled up and down several narrow streets, turning left, turning right, turning left again and careening from curb to curb. How we missed the pedestrians and merchants on both sides was beyond my understanding, but we did. Skidding to a stop at some indistinct point along the high chain-link perimeter of Camp Hansen, the driver motioned me out.

"Follow fence that way. When you see guard post, look for hole. So long."

The stars were so clear I could see through the sky. The humidity had long before soaked into my tropical uniform, meeting my sweat coming through from the other side. It was a wet, wrinkled mess. By the time I found the hole in the fence and crawled back through, planting my feet safely on U.S. territory, it was covered with mud as well. That's when the flashlight beam blinded me. Instinctively, I threw up my hands to cover my face.

"Halt. Who goes there?"

I dropped my hands to the side and assumed a rigid stance called *at attention.*

"Private First Class James McGarrah, serial number 2371586, SIR."

"Don't sir me, you fucking idiot. I work for a living just like you. The difference is I'm a sergeant on guard duty and you're AWOL."

"Yes sir. I just wanted . . ."

"I know what you wanted, asshole. You wanted to get laid before you got your dick shot off. When do you ship out for 'Nam?"

I was still standing at attention, but he had pointed the flashlight down at the ground in order to put me at ease. I realized then that he wasn't going to bust my rank, or lock me in the stockade. I guess he figured that where I was going was punishment enough.

"0800, tomorrow morning."

"You mean *this* morning. It's 0500 already. Don't think I don't know about the deals that Lance Corporal Saunders makes with you dumb fucking green-ass losers. Your problem is that his tour of duty ended three hours ago. Now, get back to your barracks and square yourself away before I decide to arrest you."

Moving away from the sergeant at a double-time pace, I heard him shout.

"Hey, numbnuts, buy a watch."

Chapter 7

HEY JOE, WHERE YOU GOIN' WITH THAT GUN IN YOUR HAND?

All myths grow from the seeds of truth. Accordingly, the Marine Corps rifleman has been almost deified throughout American military history. From the shores of Tripoli fighting pirates in the eighteenth century to the Chosin Reservoir in the frozen highlands of Korea, the individual marine and his rifle have conducted almost supernatural feats of marksmanship and bravery. Unlike the army, navy, or air force, every marine is primarily trained and can serve well as an infantry soldier. Their rifles are unique to them, an extension of their bodies, even a facet of their personalities. In November 1963 Lee Harvey Oswald shot President John F. Kennedy from a book depository window in Dallas, Texas. In August 1966, a scant year before my graduation from basic training, Charles Whitman gained his fame as the University Sniper from a clock tower in Austin, Texas. Both men learned to shoot in the Marine Corps, and if we are to believe they really made those nearly impossible hits with mediocre rifles, then we must accept the myth that a marine with a rifle is an unparalleled lethal weapon. I use the word *myth* because *fact* would be predicated on the reality that every marine got issued a rifle that actually worked. That wasn't always the case in Vietnam.

The flight from Okinawa to Da Nang took a few short hours and was fairly comfortable in the belly of a C-130 transport, where I lounged with thirty or forty other FNGs (fucking new guys) who were on the way to various units as replacements in the I Corps area of South Vietnam. The first rude push out of my comfort zone came in the form of something called an assault landing.

We flew comfortably along, the great metal bird gliding across the skyway buoyed by cushions of calm air. Then my ass was in my throat. The floor of sky dropped away as if the plane had rolled into a huge hole. We rode an unchecked elevator from the top of the clouds to the tarmac in the fastest few seconds of my life.

Pilots flying the lumbering C-130 transport planes had been instructed not to enter Da Nang air space in their normal, graceful arc, backing off the throttle gradually and setting the huge shell down gently. It took too long and who knew if the Vietcong hid in the tree line with B-40 rockets. In an ordinary landing pattern, the planes became fish in a barrel. So the pilots developed a safety precaution. They tilted the nose of the plane downward and dove at the ground at full speed until the last possible moment and then jerked the nose upward until the plane was parallel and on top of the runway. We were supposed to be told this by the pilot. He forgot. Consequently, my first real thought that I might be dying came to me above Vietnam rather than on it.

Once the plane taxied to a stop and dropped its rear ramp, I walked into the diamond-like sunlight of I Corps area as if I were Jonah disgorged from the belly of the leviathan and sent on a mission that I was becoming increasingly reluctant to fulfill. A sergeant, some rear-area office pogue, pulled us into formation.

"How many of you are O positive?" he asked. Three of us raised our hands. "Good. You're what we call universal donors. Your blood works in anybody and God knows we need it. The grunts just took a lot of casualties on operation outside of the Rockpile. That's where most of you will be going, but before you go there, we need to relieve you of a pint of your blood to help your brothers-in-arms. *Semper Fidelis*."

One of the other replacements who was O positive said, "Won't we be needing all we've got?" He meant it as a joke, but it drew only a few strained chuckles in response. The three of us reported to a tin Quonset hut just off the runway and surrounded by sandbags. The building doubled as a blood repository and a morgue. There, among the stacks of oddly shaped body bags, I laid motionless on a stainless-steel table. As a navy corpsman jammed a needle into my vein and began sucking the blood from my left arm into a sterile plastic bag, a coldness overwhelmed me and my stomach fluttered like I had just driven fast over a sharp hill, or made another assault landing.

"Are those bags full?"

"Yep."

"Why do some of them bulge in different places than others?"

"Those are the ones with pieces. Sometimes we don't get every-thing back, and sometimes it don't fit together like it used to."

The corpsman ate a sandwich, sang to the dead, and danced as if he were on stage at the Apollo with the Temptations: "I know you want to leave me, but I refuse to let you go. If I have to beg and plead for your sympathy, I don't mind 'cause you mean that much to me. Ain't too proud to beg sweet dead boys. . . ."

* * *

I spent two nights and three days in Da Nang getting rained on while my orders were processed and the officer in charge of replacements waited for someone else to die. The brilliant sun-light gave way to a steady downpour of monsoon rain late every morning. The rain went on and on and on, usually until the next morning when the sun fooled you again. I had no opportu-nity to visit China Beach or the town of Da Nang itself. I wasn't even outfitted with weapon and jungle gear. Instead, I learned a new trade, one that has proved invaluable the older I get. I was assigned shit duty. This isn't an outcropping of my tendency to think metaphorically, although it does kind of sum up the whole war. I mean I was literally given the task of dragging fifty-five gallon barrels that had been sliced in half out from under the wooden outhouses and firing up the shit. The stench of human waste bit through even the cotton balls I shoved up my nose. I thought if this stuff lived inside us no wonder we were mean. The corporal in charge of waste management gave me an asbestos glove and a five-gallon fuel tin full of diesel. I poured the fuel into each of the four barrels assigned to me, lit them, and stoked the flames with a charred stick and my asbestos hand so the fuel would seep to the bottom of the shit and burn it all.

Black smoke merged with the body of the sky. I developed a rhythm in harmony with the thumping of the artillery battery on the other side of the base. They were firing the regular morning Harassment and Interdiction mission. I learned two things later as the war unfolded in my mind: The smell of burning shit isn't as noxious to the memory as the smell of burning flesh, and H & I fire was random and indiscreet, killing far more civilians in villages than VC. But for these moments, the thump of artillery going out instead of shells whining as they came in generated a sense of security to Private First Class Jim McGarrah, serial number 2371586, Fucking New Guy, stranger in a strange land.

Evidently someone had rotated home, got himself wounded, or got greased. On the morning of the third day, the duty sergeant handed me my orders and I boarded a CH-46 helicopter for the short ride to Phu Bai. I had been assigned to a rifle platoon in Third Battalion, Ninth Marines. The unit operated out of Camp Carroll, also known affectionately as the Rockpile, in the northern reaches of South Vietnam very close to the demilitarized zone. The Ninth Marines had seen some action, earning a reputation as tough, efficient killers, and I believed I had been given a prime spot to participate in the war. Phu Bai was the huge rear base where I would be supplied with my jungle equipment and my first M-16. I had trained primarily with the 7.62 millimeter M-14, and felt anxious to get my hands on this new and, according to the military brass that bought them, magical weapon.

I don't remember many particulars about Phu Bai. My mind was fogged with new sensations, sights, smells, tastes, and sounds. People drifted in and out of this fog like shadows of trees and I made very little contact. This was one of the paradoxes of Vietnam, maybe of all war. Under fire, I met men who became instantly closer to me than brother or lover because all of us depended on each other for our lives. At the same time, the closeness remained buffered by a numbness that disallowed any real meaning to the word *intimate* because the man next to you could disappear in the flash of a rocket or the thud of a bullet.

The supply sergeant at Phu Bai, however, is clearly fixed in my psyche still, maybe even more so after thirty years, as a fat asshole with froglike eyes, black hair, a nasal twang, and pug nose, who smelled of urine and had the habit of drooling all over a cheap cigar he chewed. Why am I so clear? I spent my first few days with a combat unit thinking about how I could kill him for giving me my first M-16.

Like every other morning since I had arrived in country, the sun burned with white heat in its illusion of a beautiful day before the rain began. I squinted blindly walking into the cool, airy shadows of the cavernous supply hut. The frog-faced fat-ass sergeant smiled at me across a long counter. For a moment, blue clouds of cigar smoke hanging over the man's head created a twinge of homesickness. I thought of my father in his office puffing away at a Dutch Masters and reading the *Daily Racing Form*.

"Welcome to hell, boy," said the sergeant. "I'm the gatekeeper. Whadda you want?"

"I'm going to the Rockpile."

"Well then, you'll damn sure need one of these." He held up a Louisville Slugger baseball bat. "They'll stick fresh meat like you out on point one night and you'll run into a rock ape. Little fellers, but mean. They'll throw you off a cliff quicker than snot." He laughed and I thought it was all a big joke, so I laughed as well. When I got to my squad later that day, I found out the man I replaced had a dislocated shoulder and a broken collarbone. A rock ape met him on the trail during a routine night patrol. The marine reached out to shoo the animal away quietly and the ape threw him over its shoulder and down an embankment like a Japanese judo master.

Sergeant Froggy put the bat back under the counter and reached behind him to a shelf full of jungle boots.

"These are size nine," I said.

"Yep. You can read."

"I wear size eight."

"Not any more. Size nine is all we got left. Everybody wears size nine."

The rest of my visit went the way it began. I got a rain poncho and field jacket without their liners, which became a severe problem on listening post at night in the mountains when temperatures dropped to forty-five degrees and I was soaking wet from the monsoons. I don't remember ever being colder than on those nights. "It's a tropical country. You don't need no liners," said Froggy. He handed me a mess kit without utensils, a helmet with no plastic liner so it hung uselessly over my eyes, and a canteen with a bullet hole. The flak jacket seemed to be intact, so I put it on, but the zipper was broken and it left my heart exposed. Finally, he unlocked the weapons locker and gave me the M-16. Lithe and light, its black plastic stock comfortable in my grip, I worked the bolt back and forth. The action was smooth and solid. With that rifle in my hands, like my poet-warrior ancestors from the Celtic highlands and their claymore swords, I felt ready to meet the enemy. The rest of the gear I should have gotten, or did get only partially, proved to be a minor irritant even when I found out a few hours later from a drunken mess cook that the sergeant was selling the jacket and poncho liners and the new canteens on the black market. I had already begun to shed that innocence that shrouds young men who grow up narrow and privileged in America's heartland. As long as I had a weapon though, I would be okay.

The truck convoy to the Rockpile took several hours out of that same day. None of the drivers seemed overly concerned that we sat in the back of an open truck vulnerable to snipers and land mines. Since early 1967, when the 324B North Vietnamese Army regiment had been driven from the immediate countryside, the whole section of territory along Route 9 that surrounded Camp Carroll, or firebase Rockpile, proved relatively secure. This intelligence information meant nothing to me. As we rolled past the gnarled old women in the doorways of their hooches, I watched them pick through the knotty hair of their vacant-eyed children, find the lice one at a time, and then crush them between their teeth, rotted and blackened by years of chewing betel nut. I suspected every woman I saw, even the ones shitting in the rice paddies or carrying tins of water, of being VC. As an American, I felt sure that no good, God-loving human could act this uncivilized.

I want to say I was frightened, but that isn't accurate. I felt curious and alert the entire trip. All the childish years of watching American soldiers win in war movies, of playing sports and praying in huddles for the death of my opponents, of listening to television news chatter about the evils of Communism, of hearing the stories of sacrifice and honor from the World War II vets who drank coffee every day in the Palace Pool Room, and that one crushing hammer of rejection from the all-American cheerleader, brought me to this time and place and gave me a childish attitude toward war. I felt chosen to be here by some force beyond my control. I felt immortal. I could see the same pumped-up adrenaline rush on the clean-shaven faces of the other replacements riding in the open truck bed who, like me, had never been under enemy fire. Meanwhile, the few marines who had been in-country for several months either stared silently into the distant tree line as if waiting for something ugly but inevitable, or dozed off beneath the blue silk sky. No one spoke much except for groans of discomfort in perfect rhythm with the truck bouncing over pock-marked and shell-shocked asphalt. I think it was because the FNGs like me didn't know what to say and the short-timers returning to the firebase after R & R knew that out there along the DMZ words were useless. However, I remember one corporal who was sleeping had written these words on his helmet, "When I die I'll go to heaven because I've spent my time in hell."

*   *   *

The name Rockpile had no hidden meaning that I could tell. It was an image that translated the reality of my new home perfectly. Our supreme military commander General William Westmoreland, in all his idiotic glory, had decided that the path to victory in Vietnam lay in the tactic of attrition. I didn't fully understand the meaning of attrition then, only that the Marine Corps had been charged by him with the task of creating a series of interlocking firebases across the top of South Vietnam and then, from these firebases, killing the NVA that was moving across the DMZ until there weren't any more of them. That the task was impossible, or that attrition was a two-way street, never occurred to the great general from the safety of his Saigon palace. So the Corps built ten firebases beginning with Dong Ha twelve miles south of the DMZ and twelve miles west of the eastern coast. After Dong Ha came Cam Lo. Both bases occupied flat ground and had clear fields of fire.

The terrain rose into jagged ridgelines the further west you went. The Rockpile was third in line, no longer flat but rather seven hundred feet of black rock surrounded alternately by dense jungle and napalm-charred cinders. Initially, I thought I had been transported to the dark side of the moon. After dismounting from the truck, I found a lance corporal in the motor pool willing to lead me to the sandbagged bunker that served as command post for my platoon. I entered and presented my orders to First Lieutenant Ronald Jermakowitz, whose shaved head bowed over a laminated map on the desktop.

Jermakowitz pushed his chair back and began to stand as I came to rigid attention on the opposite side of the desk. The air in the bunker was cool but claustrophobic and smelled like wet dirt. I imagined a grave and being buried alive.

"At ease, son." The lieutenant stood now and towered over me like a giant tree. I had been almost too short at five feet, six inches, to pass the physical when I enlisted, but this man unfolded at least a foot past the top of my head. He had a slight scar radiating from his upper lip that made him seem to be constantly sneering at you. Even in the relatively casual atmosphere of his bunker, he wore a complete uniform. The sleeves on his olive-drab jungle fatigues were rolled high enough that a bulldog tattoo stared at me from his left bicep. Under the ugly dog the words "Death Before Dishonor" were scrawled with blood-colored ink. As he leaned into my face, I smelled whiskey on his breath so strong that even his Old Spice couldn't mask it.

"I'm a mustang officer. Do you know what that is?"

"You came up through the enlisted ranks, sir."

"Precisely. That means I know how to work for a living and I expect my men to keep up with me, or die trying."

"Yes sir."

Walking over to the doorway, Jermakowitz called out some corporal's name who he introduced as my squad leader. I remember neither the name nor the man's face, only that he seemed exhausted and hollow.

"Take PFC McGarrah to your area and then assemble the squad at the rifle range. I want a weapons check before we leave tomorrow."

On the way across camp to stow my gear, I asked my squad leader where we were going tomorrow.

"Another one of Lieutenant Jerksilly's stingray patrols."

"What's that?"

"You'll see if you last long enough."

* * *

The rifle range proved to be little more than a flat area of blanched dust and rusted, useless equipment. It looked very much like an American salvage yard and could have passed easily for one in Detroit or Chicago, especially with the staccato bursts of rifle fire and the stench of gunpowder. I aimed at a dead jeep. The explosion was sweet and a feeling of power surged through my arms like electric current. I aimed at the jeep again, already mortally wounded by a mortar shell, and squeezed the trigger for the second time. Nothing. I squeezed it again. Nothing again. I reached down and worked the bolt manually. The empty brass cartridge flew out of the chamber and another round settled into it. I fired. Nothing. I squeezed the trigger the second time. Nothing. I felt like a kid under the Christmas tree on Christmas morning who expects to unwrap his present and find a train set, but finds instead a bow tie to wear in church. I motioned for my new squad leader.

"Corporal, this rifle's jamming after one round."

He shrugged his shoulders and said, "I'll send the lieutenant over when he gets here. Until it gets fixed, stay away from me when we go on patrol."

He had no reason for concern. I had no intention of leaving the safety of the concertina wire, the minefield around it, and the 155 artillery pieces without a fully functioning weapon. When Jermakowitz moved down the firing line to my position, I told him the dilemma. He jerked the rifle away from me and fired a round.

"It works fine, private."

"It's got a gas leak or something. It won't chamber another round."

"This is a tough outfit and my men don't complain. We suffer for America. Pain is good. Are you complaining, pussy?"

"No sir."

"Then clean your rifle good and make the first shot count. Be a Marine."

* * *

The next morning, I went on my first patrol with a broken rifle. I had been in the Corps long enough to know that further argument with an officer would get me labeled as a troublemaker and every piece of shit duty that popped up would be given to me until I died. As we floated through the barbed wire like ghosts and disappeared into heavy mountain mist, I experienced my first real infection of terror. It comes on you like a virus during times of anticipation. You expect an ambush, a pungi stick, a bouncing betty, maybe just one sniper looking for an idiot to kill, so every

step through the bamboo and elephant grass intensifies the waiting until your imagination feels like it's on fire with fever, your
stomach rolls like a small boat in a storm that's ready to capsize,
and then nothing happens. You carry the sickness back to the base
at the end of the day and medicate it with a Thai stick, a bowl of
hash, or a bottle of whiskey, maybe all three. If it's your night for listening post and you know there will be a time out in the blackness
alone when all the jungle sounds stop at once, when the toucans,
the rock apes, the vipers, the bats, and the bugs all quit breathing
in unison, maybe you swallow a couple of amphetamines so you
can at least hear your own heart racing in the vacuum.

By the end of a week's worth of these stingray patrols, where
Jermakowitz ran us up and down mountains and through jungle
so thick it took hours to cut a few meters of pathway to "keep us
sharp," and two night-duty listening posts with a rifle that wouldn't
work, I was emotionally and physically exhausted. All I could think
of every waking hour was the fat supply sergeant's face. With my
nerves frayed like worn cable, I could see him in my mind, drinking his warm beers from the PX, jacking off in the shithouse with
his new issue of *Playboy*, sleeping soundly in his air-conditioned
tent like a fat bear in winter, and all I wanted to do was put the
barrel of my M-16 between his bushy eyebrows, gently squeeze the
trigger, and smile as my one and only shot lifted the back of his
head away from the skull.

Fortunately for both of us, the platoon suffered a casualty without making enemy contact. The radio man in third squad forgot
to take either his weekly orange pill or the daily dose of little white
ones and came down with malaria. There was some speculation
that he had forgotten on purpose. But no one proved it and no
one would have blamed him anyway because his rotation date back
to the world, as I had learned to call home, was still seven months

away. His chances of making seven months carrying the PRC-25 radio in full view of enemy snipers were almost nonexistent. Jermakowitz brought me the radio man's M-16 and had mine sent back to supply.

"Just in case you're not as stupid as you look, asshole."

Having a weapon that I could actually use to defend myself boosted my confidence. The infection of terror began to wane, replaced by a deadly curiosity about getting shot at. The supply sergeant occupied less of my thoughts. I began looking forward to patrols and the sound of Jermakowitz's deep voice as he ran up and down the line chanting, "Pain is good, motherfuckers. Pain is good." After a month of routine, the whole battalion received orders to run a search-and-destroy operation between Rockpile and Khe Sanh, which was another firebase a short distance west and which was eating a big shit sandwich made from NVA artillery shells.

Chapter 8

CONTACT

One summer a couple of years after my discharge from the Marine Corps, I traveled east to visit an old friend and Vietnam veteran named Jimmy Hayes who was a student at Boston University. We were both crazed in those days, jammed up with free love, good dope, and bad memories. On Independence Day, Hayes suggested we drive to Rye Beach in New Hampshire, get drunk, and get laid by some of the blue-blooded babes who would be lounging on the sand with their prep-school boyfriends and who would want to screw stone-cold killers to satisfy a curious morbidity in their spoiled little brains. It was a good idea and we did just that.

The reason I bring it up at this juncture in my little war story is because I'm trying to remember what it felt like to be in that first firefight, to bust my cherry as the saying goes, and this is the closest sensory perception I can recall. Hayes and I each bought a fifth of Beefeaters gin, a bag of ice, and a bottle of tonic water at one of the state-owned liquor stores close to the beach. Dragging an old army blanket across the hot sand, we set up camp in an area infested with bikini-clad prospects and went to work on the gin. The sounds of Crosby, Stills, and Nash drifted hypnotically from a nearby boom box and mingled in the air somewhere over our heads with the smells of coconut oil, Coppertone, lime juice, and expensive perfume: "Where are you going now my love, where will you be tomorrow? Will you bring me happiness, will you bring me sorrow? All the questions of a thousand dreams, what you do and what you seem . . . Carry on, love is coming . . . love is coming to us all."

As I entered a state of limbo somewhere between environmentally induced numbness and gin-induced catatonia, Hayes had the audacity to speak.

"Man, my brain is fried. That sun's a bitch."

"It's July, man."

"Yeah, but it's New Hampshire, man."

"So?"

"So that's one of the things New England's noted for."

"Summer?"

"Not just summer. We got puritans, witches, maple syrup, and *mild* summers." He stood, sweat soaked and half drunk, and poured a huge puddle of baby oil mixed with iodine across his broad and hairy chest. Rubbing it in, he stared with the vacant glare that so many of us brought home from the war out over the green ocean and into its vanishing point.

"What's on your mind?"

"You mean what's left of my mind? Swim or drown."

Rushing across the sand like the innocent children we had once been, hopping and skipping to avoid the white fire that tortured our soles, we left the earth and dove into the frosting-capped surf at full speed.

The frigid wave hit me as if I had been smashed in the chest by an open throttle locomotive. My lungs collapsed. My skin was stabbed by thousands of tiny red needles. My heart thumped loudly in my ears and beat so fast that the thumping almost became a constant hum. I clawed toward the surface, sobered and overwhelmed with a sense of dread that something totally unlike anything else had been done to me without my permission, beyond my control. I knew I was dying. When I finally broke the surface, the few seconds that had passed seemed like hours. My whole body glowed crimson. I couldn't speak and I wanted to cry. The pain was nonexistent, and yet the pain seemed horrific, more than I could bear.

"Take a breath, dumb ass. You're in shock. I forgot to tell you this is the point where some big arctic current runs closest to the coast. You'll get used to it," Hayes said, and he was right.

*　*　*

We got the order to mount up for Operation Lancaster. After four weeks in country without enemy fire except a few stray mortar rounds, I was confident and easy about this war game, especially since we'd had no casualties other than heat and exhaustion on any of Lieutenant Jermakowitz's stingray patrols. Oh, he called in air strikes and artillery strikes at every opportunity. He slaughtered trees, bamboo shoots, and patches of elephant grass with sadistic pleasure. Occasionally, the idiot would mix up map coordinates and walk the 155 howitzer rounds right next to our position on some hilltop or ridgeline we'd been forced to hump up and dig in for his pretend war. Shrapnel, dirt, and rocks would rain down on our helmets around the makeshift perimeter and the lieutenant would laugh. The thing was, no one had ever shot back, and that lulled me in to believing we had already won the war. I packed my gear for this search-and-destroy operation like I planned a hike in the woods with the Boy Scouts. Of course, I forgot the difference between the Scouts and the Corps. The Boy Scouts had adult leadership.

I picked up my flak jacket, and then a bandolier with twelve magazines for the M-16, and slung them both over my shoulder, not because I thought they might be useful, but because I thought they looked cool and someone might take a picture I could send home. Hooking four M-20 fragmentation grenades and two smoke grenades into loops on the flak jacket, I then stuck a green pop-up

Tunnel rat, DMZ, 1967.

flare in the deep pocket on the side of my fatigues and stuffed a field dressing and a plastic bottle of insect repellant in the rubber band on my helmet.

Napalm and Agent Orange had burned most of the thick jungle away around the huge base camp, so I ignored the machete. It would just be useless weight and it irritated me banging against my leg when Jermakowitz forced us up hills at double time. Lastly, I dropped two Halizone tablets in my new canteen (I had to buy one from the Vietnamese black marketeer to replace the one with a hole given me by the froggy supply sergeant) to purify the water, then emptied a package of grape Kool-Aid into it as well. There was no way to get past the bitter taste of Halizone without grape Kool-Aid.

I hooked the canteen on my belt and checked the musty bunker that had become my home to make sure nothing useful had hidden in the folds of dirty T-shirts or under the blanket on my cot. Three other marines shared this place with me, including a pudgy lance corporal named Williams from Missouri who was the fire-team leader and who everyone called Sheep because he claimed to fuck farm animals back home. He said they didn't talk back like women. A pasty private first class from Harrisburg, Pennsylvania, named Dimkovski slept in the cot next to mine. His family had immigrated from Eastern Europe after World War II. Everyone called him Dimwit because he spoke English with a thick accent and stuttered frequently. The last member of our little sandbag co-op came from Detroit, a quiet, sullen black man who had survived two tours in 'Nam and had returned for a third. Rumor had it that Willie Mason was a stone-cold killer from the mean streets and kept coming back to the war so he could legally practice the art. His tall, lean frame and his cruel eyes gave credence to the rumors. Truth was he'd been caught shoplifting a

Supremes cassette tape from an inner-city Ben Franklin store, and a judge gave him the option of jail or a four-year enlistment. He took the enlistment. The Marine Corps had no use for him in the States and he was their prisoner, so they kept sending him back to Vietnam. Mason had that hard stare because he figured the third time was a charm. His luck had run out, in his mind.

We survived together in that claustrophobic environment because we had to. Since I was unproven in combat, the other three didn't trust me yet, so we didn't communicate much. Even on this day, they had all split for the staging area without me. I can't say that the mistrust was a one-way street. I hadn't been under fire with them either, and until I felt confident they had my back, a tension would remain between us. Also, part of their paranoia came from smoking too much dope and part came from understanding the law of averages, especially Mason. He'd spent over two-and-a-half years with a combat unit and had never been hit. After that long, anyone could appreciate that fate had skated by once too often. Still, I knew that Mason in particular had reached a mental saturation point and was looking for a way out because he voiced that concern every time he got stoned. In my mind this made him the most unreliable.

Since I had yet to enter their world of terror and smoke I remained skeptical of their sincerity regarding the great American effort to bring democracy to an ignorant peasant nation. I instinctively shrugged my shoulders, blew a kiss to Sheep's poster of Janis Joplin that hung on the wall, dragged my tired ass into the Vietnamese sunlight, joined my unit, and began to hope this was the day I would meet Victor Charlie.

Once we cleared the perimeter, each man checked his weapon and took the safety off. Locked and loaded, we joined a loose formation of squads in the four platoons from Company B. The captain's philosophy was safety in numbers for as long as possible. Our platoon humped and sweated, silent and alert for almost two kilometers, and then broke away from the company to find our assigned killing zone. My fire team took the point. We spread out into a "V" formation with Dimkovski in the lead. Sheep trailed on his left about three meters behind, and Mason and I followed the same distance on the right. Jermakowitz ordered all new guys on point until they were blessed with the first firefight. His rationale was logical enough. If the new guy lived, he would gain wisdom and experience. If he died, Jermakowitz wouldn't have wasted a marine who was already combat tested. So, for the last three weeks' worth of stingray patrols, my fire team had been training me how to look for signs, follow trails, uncover booby traps, and trip ambushes. It was the single most important and most dangerous job on patrol. Sheep, Mason, and Dimkovski all hated the lieutenant because of this, but they accepted their role as educators with a stoic resignation and plodded on.

At noon Dimkovski led us through a small patch of elephant grass, bamboo, and banyans about five hundred meters west of Route 9. When we entered the light jungle, Sheep followed the hand signals and carefully steered the platoon parallel to the trail, but just off it. Mason smiled like a child who has outsmarted his mother at the cookie jar and whispered that the dinks believed Americans to be lazy, always taking the path of least resistance. They kept trails through the jungle clean and cultivated, giving the marines an easy walk. They also kept them well booby trapped.

Between the tree line we were in and the small rise that bordered our assigned patrol area lay a wide series of interlaced rice paddies, a checkerboard of green and black squares. When the squad reached them, Dimkovski signaled for everyone to fan out in a firing line, hidden by the last few rubber trees in the jungle.

Normally, he wouldn't have hesitated. He had patrolled this area several times before and knew that, between where we were and where we were going, there was no cover, no place for an ambush. It was all open squares of stagnant water crisscrossed by small dikes. The VC didn't mine it because they didn't want to tear the rice up and go hungry.

Today, however, the world around him was out of kilter. He seemed agitated that no farmer worked the paddies and it was the middle of the day. Not a single child or woman from either of the two nearby villages could be seen squatting for a shit. The quiet outside him roared inside him. I could hear it in my own fear. He waved his arm for Mason to come over.

"Take McGarrah and cross the paddies. When you get to the top of the hill, check the other side of the road for movement. And be fucking careful. I don't like the fact that no slopeheads are working the rice."

"Fuck you. The dinks know something or they'd be here. I ain't taking douche bag out in the open where he might get me killed. You do it."

Dimkovski crawled down the line and conferred with Jermakowitz, who nodded his head and then came back, motioning for me to follow. He seemed disoriented, but stood and stepped out of the trees. I joined him and we made our way slowly, stopping every few meters to kneel and look in all directions. Jermakowitz had the M-60 machine gun moved right about twenty meters to create a good angle for cover fire if necessary. The heat came off the water in shimmering patches and it made the whole earth move, slithering toward the blue sky as if the sky were a whirlpool swallowing up the dirt, the water, and everything attached to me. I felt drunk and seasick as I watched the air shimmy and shake, like I might vomit. What a time to have a nervous breakdown. Was I really this chicken shit? I lifted off my helmet and wiped the sweat from my eyes.

Nothing happened. We reached a small hill beyond the paddies and climbed it. Jermakowitz moved the rest of the platoon double-time over the paddies. They stopped at the foot of the low incline and he passed the word down that we could drink and eat, but not light cook fires. The men spaced themselves evenly apart in a small perimeter and began to catch their breath. After placing lookouts on the flanks, the lieutenant waved us in to join Mason and Sheep and have lunch.

Anyone who has ever eaten a can of Spam understands about lunch on a Marine Corps operation in the jungle. C rations came in olive green cans labeled with various flavors—ham and eggs, meat loaf, turkey and dressing—but with one unique taste, cold, old lard. The longer I spent in country and the more I ate C-rats, the more I developed recipes that made them palatable. I had my mother send me Tabasco sauce, olive oil, oregano, and several other spices to add to my meals. I learned to mix certain entrees and fry the stale bread in oil with heat tabs. This particular day was a good one for me. My boxed meal contained a can of pound cake and a can of peaches, along with a small package of four Pall Mall cigarettes. I ate with good appetite and then buried the cans by digging a hole. We all did that, not because we felt environmentally conscious— after all, we had destroyed most of the country already with Agent Orange and napalm but because Charlie used the metal cans to make booby traps if he could find them. The ground was still wet from monsoon season, and although it hadn't rained yet today, my entrenching tool cut through the black earth easily. Mason and I lit cigarettes. Sheep and Dimkovski argued about whether Vietnamese hookers had slanted pussies. We waited for the order to move out and sweep another section of jungle just in front of us. It came.

We took our places. Sheep's turn on point began. Mason mentored me on this day and thus wasn't required to actually take the lead of our fire team. The rain started to parachute down in slow, wide drops as we approached another tree line, and Sheep disappeared. Since that instant in time when Sheep became a myth, a mass of sculpted muscle smoking like a sandalwood joss stick, an abstract illusion of humanity, there have been perfect machines in the forests of my mind and metal, hard lines and dark shadows destroying the beautiful, uneven symmetry of living things.

The trees dipped and swirled with the monsoon breeze. The bamboo played a tango so hypnotic and hollow I hardly noticed the other whistle, the harsh hiss of an RPG ripping through the melody like off-key fusion jazz. Sheep must have heard it, though, because he opened his arms wide and embraced the rocket. It entered him and became him, sending all unnecessary attachments in different directions. Arms flew east and west and his head shot skyward as if it were a basketball some referee had tossed for the opening jump. Damp grit splattered my fatigues and face. It felt like wet sand, but I learned later when I washed in the Ben Hoi River that it was his blood and bone.

"You hit?" Mason's voice entangled the other sounds in my mind, giving the whole scene a surreal edge, as if I watched a 3-D movie without the glasses. As a matter of fact, every firefight after this one generated that same out-of-body feeling. I was outside myself, watching myself in animated and slowed time. There were days after this when I had that feeling without being in actual combat.

"I don't think so," I said uncertainly.

"Then let's fucking get some, get some, get some for Sheep."

I thought Mason had completely lost his mind. He stood and, firing his M-16 in short bursts on full automatic from his hip, walked directly toward the trees. I screamed, "Take cover." From my dirt-hugging, prone position, I looked left and right. The entire platoon, some fifty men, had come on line with Willie and walked toward the dense undergrowth, rifles exploding in staccato bursts like a thousand insane typewriters clacking away in an unknown and unknowable language, M-79 grenade launchers thumping like bass drums in a lunatic marching band, M-60 machine guns ripping through the humid air as if it were burlap. The noise made me want to burrow into the earth and lie there forever. Then I felt Jermakowitz's foot in my ass. He stood behind me yelling as loud as he could, "Pain is good, motherfucker, pain is good." My mind shut off. It must have. Why else would I have risen and joined my comrades, taking my place in the death wall, waiting to fall, biting the trees, and watching the trees bite back?

In that firefight, two other marines were wounded and six Vietcong irregulars ended up dead, maybe more. Six was the number of bodies we found, but more drag marks and blood vanished after a few meters into the jungle. We searched for tunnel openings, but found only four well-fortified bunkers, which I crawled into and then rooted around in hoping to find documents or weapons left behind. They were empty. In a way, I was kind of sad. Juiced by the firefight, I volunteered to become the platoon's tunnel rat, which had been Sheep's job. I wanted the fire in my blood to stay there. The euphoria felt like nothing I had ever felt before, and the thought of getting face to face in a narrow space with another man and only the truest warrior surviving juiced me further. I began to understand the stupid, macho bullshit desperation of that feeling only after I had entered the darkness of three more tunnels. I discovered a Russell's viper tied to the ceiling in one just before it tried to bite me, one of our own grenades armed underneath a broken AK-47 and a stinking, cold corpse in another. Then, the fear that my luck would run out overwhelmed me in the third tunnel. I took up the practice of tossing a grenade into the opening before I descended, like Dante, into my own little claustrophobic hell.

This day, the day of Sheep's disassembly, was the exact moment in Vietnam I started the process of losing my sanity. Every combat marine does. The lunacy manifests itself in different ways like drug addiction, unnecessary risk taking, attempted fragging, rape, excessive masturbation, murder, hearing Jimi Hendrix play "Purple Haze" when there is no radio, or talking to someone and being unable to tell if they're dead or alive. But the symptoms are always similar. First, superstition becomes an obsession. You cling, like a drowning man, to an object—a rabbit's foot, prom queen's garter, photo of your sister, flask, pipe, baseball card, Zippo lighter, Swiss army knife, pair of rotting socks, hat, Saint Christopher medal, silver cross, Con-Tikki, dashiki, bracelet, necklace made from human ears, severed finger, or any of a hundred other small items—and the object becomes sacred, a talisman that guards you against death. As long as you carry it you remain invisible. You believe Death can't see you. I chose a worn Zippo lighter and refused to go anywhere without it. Second, your eyes develop a blank, ceramic glaze that some call "the thousand-yard stare" because people with talismans like yours die horribly around you all the time and your mind secretly knows that the reason you don't rests not in your lucky charm, but rather in the fact your soul is already dead and the body just hasn't caught up.

With the smell of cordite and gunpowder still heavy in the air, Mason and Dimkovski unwrapped a poncho and began looking for pieces of Sheep to ship back in the medavac chopper. I helped and we found most of him. My hands shook as I picked up an arm. I should have been horrified and terrified. Instead, my euphoria continued. I felt higher than I ever felt in my later life back home, even when I got hooked on amphetamines, better than when I snorted coke, clearer than when I dropped acid or mescaline. I had been injected with the primal drug Darwin described as "survival." I had played the ultimate game and won. I was ready to speak in tongues and walk on water.

This may be the reason we keep having wars, not national sovereignty, not oil, not land, not race, not even religion. No one feels more alive and outside the banality of plain old existence than when surrounded by violent, random death. No matter what moral convictions you live by, and I have come to believe that war is the most immoral of all behavior, the drug of man-to-man, in-your-face combat is addictive. The withdrawal, along with the guilt that accompanied it, when I went back home almost destroyed me.

* * *

We spent three more weeks in the field without making any contact. When the platoon finally staggered back into the Rockpile, leech infested, filthy, pissed off, and exhausted, Private First Class McGarrah was no longer a fucking new guy, but a fellow warrior. I burned leeches off my legs with a cigarette, took a hot shower that lasted two hours, and brushed my teeth six times. Ch-46D helicopters flew in a hot Thanksgiving meal for the battalion. The waiting game. I got care packages from home filled with stale cookies from my mother, pipe tobacco, the local newspapers, and words of advice from my father. In the bunker, Dimkovski and Mason smoked joints soaked in liquid opium and nodded to sleep during most of the daylight hours. I refused, still burdened by a puritanical upbringing and the fear that some god might punish me for being stoned at the precise moment the enemy chose to hit the wire. Rumors abounded that NVA regulars had come back to the area.

We heard Khe Sahn was under siege by enemy artillery just up the road and believed it was due to be overrun. Marines died there daily. We cleaned our weapons, wrote letters of love to girls we barely knew, crawled out past the wire in the black night when our turn came for listening-post duty. At the very end of November, Dimkovski took his five-day rest and recuperation leave and flew to Bangkok, Thailand, via military transport. He promised to fuck three whores at once in memory of us. We wondered if he'd bother coming back.

The day he left, Mason and I shared night watch in a shallow trench on the western perimeter, facing Khe Sahn. The moon hung high and full like a white grape. The wind howled off the DMZ and ran along the barren ground rattling the swirls of concertina wire. With the foliage burned off and in the moonlight, the barbed concertina wire looked like tumbleweed blowing across the Texas panhandle, and I got the feeling I was in the movies again. This time, I waited in the fort for the hordes of wild Indians to come and take my scalp. Crawling out twice to check the claymore mines propped in front of our trench line, I made sure Charlie hadn't reversed them in the dark shadows. No use getting seven hundred and fifty steel ball bearings in your face when you hit the hell box and blew the C-4 trying to eviscerate Victor Charlie. Our faces were covered in soot and we smelled like the diesel fuel that fired our smudge pots inside the bunker behind us.

"I can't take this anymore," said Mason.

"Take what? The bad food, the jungle rot, the rain? The fact that Dimwit is getting laid in Bang the Cock Thailand?"

Mason stood and stared out beyond our field of fire into some distant vanishing point where all things converge into one thing.

"You better get your ass down. Just because you're black doesn't mean you're invisible. Some gook sniper may be waiting to waste you."

Mason lit a cigarette. "It's my third tour, man, my third mother-fucking tour. Mother Green is gonna keep sending me back here till I die. That's the plan. That's been the plan all along. There ain't no place for a nigger in the world. The white man is gonna keep me down till he kills me."

"I'm white, motherfucker."

"No, you ain't white yet. You're a dumb cracker who's still a baby and don't have no idea how the world works. You still think this war might be about something."

"It is."

"Is it? Ask ole Sheep what it's about."

"Sheep's dead."

"My point exactly. And that's what this war's all about, death and mayhem and destruction. All the evil there is in hell don't match the evil we got right here. And by the way, if you want to know a white man, Jermakowitz is the Man. Time for him to pay up."

"Pay what?"

"So long, Cracker."

Mason climbed out of the trench and disappeared into the bunker behind me, reappearing with a dark, baseball-sized object in his hand. I heard him singing softly as he walked away from me and toward Jermakowitz's command post bunker. "Purple Haze is in my brain, lately things don't feel the same. Acting funny but I don't know why. 'Scuse me while I kiss the sky." The night closed around him.

I never saw Willie Mason again. The object in his hand was an M-20 fragmentation grenade. He entered the lieutenant's bunker without asking permission, screamed "pain is good motherfucker" and pulled the pin. The spoon flew and the four-second fuse inside burned as Mason set the grenade on Jermakowitz's desk.

Rumor has it that Mason came to attention and saluted. Some say the lieutenant pissed his pants. Others say he fainted with fright. I don't know if that's what really happened because the two of them were alone. This I know for sure. Of the several dozen M-20 grenades I saw thrown and threw myself during firefights, none failed to explode. The only dud I ever heard about came from Mason's assignment of grenades. It was his luck. The military police cuffed him and escorted him away from his visibly shaken platoon commander. Jermakowitz kept the unexploded grenade on his desk as a good-luck charm till he was gut shot and died during Tet. I found this out from Dimkovski, who ended up in the same hospital ward as me at Cam Rahn Bay. My old infantry platoon had been wiped out. Dimwit and two FNGs were the only survivors. In my mind the bullet that took Jermakowitz just balanced the scales for the grenade that didn't.

I have no idea how much time Mason spent on the nut farm for trying to commit suicide, or how much time he spent in prison for trying to frag an officer. But Willie Mason got his wish. He went home to stay.

Chapter 9

CAG

"Never volunteer for anything," my dad warned me before I left for boot camp. I had already volunteered to be a tunnel rat—why would I hesitate when the next opportunity presented itself? Grunt work wasn't my cup of tea. I didn't like hiking through the jungle with Lieutenant Jermakowitz because I didn't trust him after the Willie Mason episode. I figured he would figure that his luck had been used up. Overly cautious men are more dangerous than crazy ones when the shit hits. Also, I wanted to stay away from as many tunnels as possible and away from the possibility that someone would mix up coordinates on an operation and call an air strike in on my head. The platoon had suffered enough casualties and rotations that all four squads were manned by brand-new replacements. Very few grunts with combat experience were left. Another high-level danger factor. So when the lieutenant called us all together and announced that a dangerous assignment to one of the new Combined Action Groups had opened up, I jumped at the chance without even knowing what a CAG unit was.

There are always advantages to being a leaper instead of a thinker. I received a meritorious promotion to lance corporal and ten days out of the field in Da Nang, where I went to classes in intelligence gathering, counterterrorism, bomb disposal, language, and Vietnamese customs and history. In the evenings I took a special course of study in international relations with the hookers around the base.

General Lew Walt, the highest-ranking marine in Vietnam, had just bought into a theory called pacification that could have won the war in 1962. That was almost six years earlier. It would turn into too little, too late during my tour, like most of the decisions that were made by upper-level staff officers in Vietnam. This historical fact was already in evidence in early December 1967. Only arrogant idiots would believe that ten days would be long enough to teach teenaged American boys all they needed to know about counterterrorism and the culture of a determined enemy. I'm guessing here, but I'd say Walt probably figured that since we were marines, on-the-job training would complete the schooling or kill us if we were too dumb to learn. Either way, we'd graduate.

Pacification meant basically doing to rice-farming peasants what the VC had been doing to them for decades, only in a kinder, gentler way. Unlike the Phoenix program, in CAG we could assassinate VC only if we could prove they were living in our particular village. We could torture them only if we said our Vietnamese counterparts did it. Everyone else, we were supposed to treat like little brothers and sisters. Theoretically, this would convince them that America was a great democratic country that burned their hamlets, destroyed their crops, killed their children, and poisoned their future generations with Agent Orange because we loved them and wanted them to experience freedom as we did.

Initially I bought into the hype that living with Vietnamese in their villages and hamlets might be the only way we could overturn the influence of their own communist countrymen and relatives. I clung to the notion that the greatest nation on earth had a responsibility to proselytize other nations with the greatest ideas of capitalism and democracy when I left Da Nang and came to live in the village of Gia Le. I didn't realize it until I'd been with the villagers a few weeks, but I was bound to that notion by the thinnest of threads—the idea that politicians and bureaucrats always told the truth. Yes, Mason had been right. When I left for my new assignment, I still hoped this war might be about something.

This is one of the great flaws of any pacification program. If you're a person with any shred of conscience and you live with an indigenous people whose civilization is thousands of years older than yours, you begin to think that it's possible they understand life better than you do and live the way they do because it works for them. You begin to see them walk with a limp, farm the land that has become part of their souls, eat, piss, pat their children on the head, cry when a pet dies, suffer, and struggle to survive. You learn from them that they consider you not liberators, but oppressors of another kind. Unlike a soldier with an infantry unit who has been taught to kill them without remorse because they are less than human, you learn through peaceful contact that they *are* human and in many ways just like you. You begin to suffer with them and want better for them and their children. You start to realize that some of the things you've been taught by your leaders aren't true, and then you wonder why they lied. Hesitation and doubt enter your mind and force it open like a flower blooming out of season. You fight the power of doubt because trusting the enemy too far can kill you and the conflict in your mind makes you bitter. Slowly, you evolve from zealous patriot to a disillusioned romantic in dirty boots.

I know this is true because my evolution started within a few short weeks after I came to live in my village.

* * *

Spread out in a sprawling circle of tin and thatch homes, animal pens, village wells, a French schoolhouse, interlocking dirt trails, rice paddies, a Buddhist temple and two bus stops, the place we called Gia Le held ten thousand civilians within its borders. Most were rice farmers; some were schoolteachers, black marketeers, refugees from other hamlets the U.S. military had burned, or relatives of VC cadres, and a few actually were VC. The population was very poor and burdened beyond salvation by the war.

The village was split into an eastern half and a western half by Route 1, which ran into Hue close to the Citadel about a mile north. Unlike the romantic Highway 1 that runs the coastline of North America from Key West, Florida, to Bangor, Maine, this highway was a narrow ribbon of bomb-cratered cement littered with demolished buildings, burned vehicles, unmarked graves, and all the other refuse of war.

Like the village and its marketplace, the CAG compound divided itself into equal halves about a hundred meters south of the marketplace collection of three-sided stalls and roadside stands where the people sold produce and scrawny chickens. On the western side, a command bunker constructed of tin and layered with sandbags housed the commander of our small group, a sergeant from Philadelphia named Jack Martin. Martin was an ex-cop with only a few weeks left in his tour. He had been with this CAG for six months and a legend had grown up around him because he had the habit of sneaking out past the wire late at night and disappearing for hours alone. Some said he made love to the half-French schoolteacher who lived in the back of the old schoolhouse. Some said he collected ears with his K-bar knife. Others said he crawled into graveyards to desecrate the dead and terrify the VC. Martin said nothing. He just smiled cruelly and let the legend grow.

I liked him, and the reason I liked him resided in the fact that he worked the opposite end of the leadership spectrum from Jermakowitz. Martin was a noncommissioned officer, an enlisted slob the same as the rest of us. He tried to make life as easy as possible because he understood that in an isolated CAG you lived

Taking a rest at CAG School, Da Nang, 1967.

with the possibility of death every minute of every day. There was no rear-area firebase, no artillery cover or battalion in reserve. You went to sleep and woke up surrounded by ten thousand Vietnamese and the risk of being overrun without warning. Martin believed that stress to be enough. Consequently, we stood no formations, did no drills, prepared for no inspections, and sweated no physical training. We simply did our best to stay alive and he helped us.

Martin once pulled me away from a bomb shelter beneath a building and crawled in himself, even though he was six inches taller and forty pounds heavier, because he believed the risk of the doorway being booby trapped was too great to order one of his men to take the chance. Unlike Jermakowitz, he inspired in his marines the one thing that makes a good leader in combat—trust. You knew Martin wouldn't ask you to do anything he wouldn't do, and you felt like your life meant something to him.

Next to the command post, a small mess tent churned out black smoke and rancid smells when there was food to cook, which wasn't often. Mostly, everyone ate C rations fried in makeshift skillets by individual heat tabs at our own bunkers. A three-foot-deep trench bolstered by sandbags ran in a half circle around the western side from the north shoulder of Route 1 to the south shoulder. Behind the trench, two-man bunkers housed well-armed marines who could spill out the doorways to the trench in an instant and set up a devastating field of interlocking fire. In front of this and following the trench line were rows of barbed concertina wire, thick like curled hair and protecting a series of claymore mines that faced outward.

The eastern side of camp had the same basic layout except for the CP and the mess tent. In their place an ancient and intricately decorated Buddhist temple stood guard over several bunkers that at various times provided sleeping quarters for the twenty or so men from the village who made up the *Dan De*, or Popular Force militia that we were training to keep the citizens secure. The newest marines always stayed on this side with the Vietnamese. The western side of camp remained segregated, supposedly for security reasons, but mainly because the physical intimacy of the androgynous little Vietnamese with each other made most Americans uncomfortable. They often held hands walking around the compound and the village. They giggled a lot and touched each other frequently, like young girls at a slumber party.

At the north and south ends on Route 1, two watchtowers mounted with M-60 machine guns and manned twenty-four hours a day by American sentries guarded access to us via the road. Every night at curfew, huge barbed-wire gates were dragged across the asphalt and no civilian traffic was allowed through. During the day, farmers and merchants routinely traversed the camp on their way from marketplace to rice fields and back again.

Other than a few strategically placed piss tubes and a latrine, this comprised my new home. I had joined a force of forty surrounded by ten thousand, and half of those forty were Vietnamese. For all I knew at the time, the Popular Forces could have been going home at night to work for VC cadres in the village. I'm sure some did. We had only small-arms fire and our winning smiles to keep us from being overrun if and whenever the enemy chose to do so.

What I thought might be easier duty than the infantry certainly appeared to be just that. There was a barber in the marketplace, a bartender who distilled his own alcohol, three disease-free local hookers, a tailor, and our Tactical Area of Responsibility consisted of the village and immediate vicinity. I would no longer run stingray patrols for miles into heavy jungle, stay in the field for weeks at a time, or be ordered around by idiot officers. However, my father always said that no matter how thin you slice bread, it always has two sides. With the increased physical comfort of this duty came an exponentially increased risk of being killed. Firefights were more frequent on patrols. One reason for that was because we went on either patrol or night ambush every single day. Booby traps were hidden everywhere and people I bought vegetables from in the sunlight were probably the ones planting them at night. It was impossible to tell with any certainty who was friend and who was foe. And, although we didn't realize it until Tet, companies of North Vietnamese regulars had begun moving through our area at night en route to Hue. Had they desired to sacrifice some of their own as casualties, the NVA could have wiped us out easily. *C'est le guerre.*

Chapter 10

OH, I WAS SO MUCH OLDER THEN

I learned the neighborhood quickly and got back to walking point. It was the only place on patrol that I felt any control at all over my own destiny. If I made a mistake, it was my own, and my life was the one jeopardized. At least that's what I told myself.

My first real understanding of what it means to play God came on a night in early January 1968, when we did a favor for the U.S. Army. As my father always said, "Son, no good deed goes unpunished."

No one in the CAG unit, including me, should have ever run any operations for the army, but war did funny things to time and space, and most importantly to reality. Our compound was about a half mile from the huge army base camp built right after Christmas to the west of us. No one knew why it had been placed there, but it had been an amazing thing to watch all the equipment the army brought through our gates on Route 1. First, they had to build a road through Lua Nam, the dense and heavily fortified jungle that bordered our village. What the Marine Corps would have been charged to do with machetes, the army did with bull-dozers, backhoes, road graders, and cement trucks. Of course, equipment operators needed care and maintenance as well as the equipment. Following the bulldozers came trucks loaded with hot chow, cold beer, and various PX items, including but not limited to air conditioners, stereos, and electric razors.

Within a few days, a whole city rose from the cleared area. Quonset huts, tents, concrete helicopter pads, walls and wire, floodlights and sirens, a full-service bar, and a full-service hospital tent sprawled out to the edges of the jungle like urban sprawl gone mad. On the one hand, we didn't mind the close proximity of the base because the PX trucks coming through would occasionally toss off a few cases of beer and cartons of cigarettes. On the other hand, the huge base provided an excellent target and the VC came to practice with mortars and B-40 rockets like moths to a flame. That meant they were sneaking through our village at night in much greater numbers than usual, making our night patrols a lot more dangerous. Going outside the wire after dark became like playing a high-stakes poker game without much money. If we were dealt the wrong hand just once, the game was over.

On this evening at dusk an army jeep driven by some captain roared past the CAG sentry post in the village marketplace. Three members of my squad, Ron Johnson, Mac Barnett, Mike Rawlings, and I finished chewing our supper, the last of seven scrawny chickens bought from and cooked by the illustrious mayor's wife. Freddie Thomas pushed through the screen door of the mess tent.

"Why aren't you at your post asshole?" asked Rawlings, who was a corporal, my squad leader and, by virtue of seniority, second in command to Sergeant Martin.

"You ain't gonna believe this. You just ain't gonna fucking believe it."

"Believe what?" I chimed in with a mouthful of chicken.

"Some frigging army officer, drunk on his ass, just drove through the marketplace. Yelled at me that he had to get back to that country club base of theirs just outta our TAOR. I yelled back 'the road's unsecure fucker.' He tells me that he's gonna fuck my momma and keeps driving."

Barnett lit a Pall Mall from one of those complimentary packs of four cigarettes that come in boxes of C rations and laughed. When he spoke, the smoke from his mouth punctuated the first few words.

"Hell, boys, we got a double blessing. The Lord God of Holy Hosts is giving us good American Catholic boys communion." Barnett raised his right arm and flailed the air in a crosshatched pattern, chanting as he did, "Inthenameofthefather andoftheson andoftheholyghost—IbetIcanbeatyouatdominooooes." The rest of us just snorted. "Some gook sniper will off this guy's ass within the next five minutes and poof, one less officer to fuck with the enlisted. Plus, the army will run a fancy ass operation from their new country club base through here with tanks and Hueys looking for that one little sniper and we won't have to go out on patrol. We can kick back, smoke dope, and drink Nguyen's homemade rice piss for a week. A double blessing in the name of the father, the son, and the holy ghost of some officer."

"Hey stupid, a third of this country's Catholic," shouted Johnson.

"Well then, it's a gook blessing, too."

"Alright, enough bullshit. Get back on watch, Freddie," said Rawlings. "McGarrah, roust the rest of first squad. We've got patrol tonight anyway and we're going to have a mess to clean up shortly."

"Can I finish my chicken?"

"Sure, maybe that army asshole will skate through without a scratch. Hey, is that a wishbone I see in your hand?"

"You mean this thing?" I shredded the last bit of stringy chicken from the small Y-shaped breastbone.

"Don't break it."

"What do you mean, don't break it? Don't tell me you believe that shit my grandma taught me when I was a kid?"

"Hell yes, whoever gets the long half gets a free wish and the wish comes true."

"And you believe that crap after all you've seen happen over here?"

"Don't you go everywhere with that funky old Zippo in your pocket?"

I wanted to argue that I carried it to light my cigarettes, that I was intelligent and sane enough to ignore superstition. Then I remembered how my own father had once stopped the car on the way to my Little League all-star game. A black cat had run in front of us. Dad backed the car almost a mile down a gravel lane and then drove six miles out of the way to avoid crossing the cat's path. Anyone who avoids violent death when he shouldn't desperately wants to believe there's a reason why and that the reason is somehow controlled by him. I needed luck just like my father, Rawlings, and the rest of my unit.

"I didn't want to be superstitious and I wasn't, until the Rhonda Dixon incident. She was a cheerleader with blonde hair and perfect tits. Me, I was a frigging saxophone player in the high school marching band, or the White Squirrels, as we were known."

"In other words, you had no shot at all with perfect Rhonda, especially with a pussy name like White Squirrel."

"Exactly. Then my mother fixed fried chicken for my graduation dinner. Me and my little brother pulled the wishbone. I got the bigger half and I wished for just one orgasm with Rhonda."

"Did it work?"

"We had a senior keg party two nights after I got that big half of the wishbone. Rhonda was there, drunk on her ass. I was wearing Todd Jones' football jersey. Todd being the hero of the White Squirrels, Rhonda sees that jersey and, without even looking at my face, gives me the first and probably best blow job I ever had."

We pulled the bone apart. Rawlings smiled. The longer gray piece floated like driftwood in his palm. A single burst from an AK-47 interrupted the ritual. We ran out of the mess hall and next door into the command bunker where Sergeant Martin and the other squad leader named Bobby Wolfe listened to a PRC-25 radio crackle and pop.

"Tango Two Charlie, Tango Two Charlie. This is Charlie One Actual. Do you copy. Over."

From the safety of the Phu Bai CAG command, the night duty officer ordered our unit to retrieve an army jeep that had just been ambushed in our TAOR. According to the officer in charge, the driver managed to desert the jeep and run back to his base camp. There he was shot and killed by sentries because he had forgotten the password. Now the jeep was a liability because the VC could steal it and trade it back to the South Vietnamese Army for American-made mines and weapons. Because we were closest to the jeep, we had been involuntarily volunteered by some officer in Phu Bai who thought helping the army might further his career.

Rawlings told Martin that first squad was already on top of the situation because it was our night for patrol anyway. I left the bunker and, within a few minutes, had maneuvered the rest of the marines and Popular Forces from our squad into a staggered line at the front gate. Rawlings remained behind a few minutes to study the map and line up firing coordinates with the mortar crew in case we needed support. We waited, ready to move through the village and retrieve the jeep.

It had rained most of the day, but by sundown, the rain had stopped. The jungle around the compound smelled new, alive, clean. For a few seconds, as the patrol slipped into darkness out past the concertina wire, I felt surrounded by serenity. I forgot where I was and thought only of where I wanted to be. The euphoria came back, as if the air I breathed was filtered through some cosmic water pipe filled with good black hash.

Something rustled slightly in an animal pen on my left side. In one fluid motion, I flicked the selector switch on my M-16 to full automatic and whirled to meet the sound. A water buffalo grunted and found salvation in the animal snort of its exhaled breath.

The squad moved north into the marketplace, a mime troupe with black shadow makeup. Each member followed the slow-motion contortions of the man in front of him. Tri, the Vietnam-ese scout with missing front teeth and basketball head, lifted his skinny leg and lowered his foot gently into the spot mine vacated. The rationale was simple. If the point man lived to take another step, the space he stepped out of was safe. But I always believed the mimicry connected us emotionally as well. Walking in someone else's footsteps gave the group a collective strength, like linking a chain or braiding a rope.

Following Tri at one-meter intervals were Rawlings, Johnson and his radio, and two young Vietnamese cousins named Nguyen and Phuc Tran. Barnett humped the heavy M-60 machine gun. The navy corpsman Rick Santos and his trainee Li Thi trailed him. The tail-end Charlie was a tall, lean, black shadow with dead eyes who reminded me a lot of Willie Mason. Flea Chavis had already served one tour and had now survived most of another one. He handled an M-79 grenade launcher like it was a conductor's baton and could orches-trate a symphony of destruction in a few seconds. I never fully trusted the man's dull eyes because of Mason, but felt safe enough for the moment that their cold stare was directed at the mutual enemy.

Wolfe's squad waited as a reaction force at the compound. That was standard procedure, one squad outside the wire and the other squad torqued up and waiting inside to bail them out. We had a third squad, but they were specialists who operated the two mortars and did most of the sentry duty. Their job was protecting us inside the wire.

Kneeling in the shadows of the barber's thatched hut, I raised my right fist. Tri's went up immediately. The signal ran down the line and the squad fell to their knees like a row of dominoes toppling. Looking through the pale moonlight into the marketplace, the thought had come to me that death was not my worst fear. It never woke me at night or bothered my appetite. I drank rice wine and had learned to smoke an occasional Thai stick because the result made me giggle, not because it gave me courage. I kept the idea of death shrouded in the fog of disappointment. I didn't want my corpse in a casket to shatter my father's expectations. He looked so guilty at the airport saying goodbye, as if he had somehow failed to teach me that immortality was reserved for gods, not teenagers. I never once feared that instant when the conscious shuts off like a light switch, but was terrified of what that instant might mean for him.

Looking back, I wonder if that delusion embedded in my perception made me careless. When the boxlike outline of the abandoned jeep caught my eye about twenty meters in front of the squad's position in the marketplace, I stood and moved forward into the full light of the moon. The asphalt on Route 1 appeared wet beneath my feet in the brightness. I could distinguish the intricate carvings along the borders of the wood and plaster Buddhist shrine across the road, the way the craftsman's tools had dipped and dived in concentric circles to scar the wood with mystical and silent incantations, the way the artist's brush had delicately coaxed the dull gray designs into living red and gold. Suddenly, exhaustion overwhelmed me with the thought that so much beauty could coexist with so much ugliness. I wanted to get the jeep back to the compound and go to sleep as quickly as possible, even if I had to become a target to do it.

There was a single pop, a muzzle flash from the shrine in front of me, and then a gurgling sound behind me, like water being sucked down a drain. I dropped to one knee and opened up on full automatic blowing the shrine to bits. No one else fired because they were all behind me and I was in the way. After three seconds my magazine emptied and the marketplace grew silent. Then I heard the gurgling again and turned around, crawling back across the road to the rest of the squad. Rawlings rocked back and forth on one knee. His hands grasped his own throat as if he were choking himself. He dangled momentarily between life and death and then, like a marionette whose string has been cut, he flopped through the night and hit the ground with a dull thud. I reached out and touched his shirt. It was soaked with blood.

At that instant, I detected fear that transcended adrenaline. Johnson was positioned between Rawlings and a well. The radioman could see very little in the shadows of the houses. The gurgling noises must have driven him to the very edge of sanity, especially since he heard me firing at something, but no fire in return. Maybe he thought some VC had slipped up on Rawlings and slit his throat. Maybe he thought snakebite, heart attack, smallpox, or black syphilis. Maybe he believed whatever got Rawlings was contagious. All I could think was that Johnson's fear forced his hands into a single stupid act. He needed to see, to know what he did not. Before I could stop him, Johnson smacked a pop-up flare against the ground. The white ball of phosphorus shot skyward from its aluminum tube. Reaching an altitude of a hundred feet, a small parachute opened, and the blaze began to drift downward. With the flare swinging back and forth on strings, the marketplace was suddenly transformed into a huge strobe-lit dance floor. The whole squad moved in stiff, slow-motion twitches, fully exposed to enemy rifle fire.

There was none. Whoever shot at the army captain and fired once at me was long gone. By the time I could see Rawlings's body clearly, Santos had already knelt beside it and laid his fingers across our squad leader's neck searching frantically for a pulse. At first,

I had no idea what had happened, but I knew Rawlings was dead. Then, I realized the single round meant for me must have caught him—a freakish overlapping of our lucks. My lucky Zippo proved stronger than his wishbone. I fought the fear that began to close in. It wasn't the fear of death as much as the randomness of its arrival.

Santos and I picked the body up from the ground, ran to the jeep, and threw it across the hood. Barnett, close by, slammed the gearshift into neutral and got behind it with Johnson. We began to push. Chavis sent up another flare to light the way back. Any cover we had was already blown by the first flare.

The Vietnamese stayed a few meters behind us as Tri checked around the shrine for a VC body without finding one. They joined us rapidly.

"Either one of you dumb fuckers check for keys?" whispered Flea.

The keys were still in the ignition and the engine started. The whole squad piled into or onto the jeep and Barnett steered us back to the compound before the second flare hit the ground. I saw Thomas running across the road, pulling the gate open. When the jeep rolled to a stop in front of the mess tent, I checked his watch. Sixteen minutes had passed since I led the patrol out, yet I felt like I'd been boxing in a sauna room for hours.

Chavis and Barnett lifted Rawlings's body from the jeep, carried it into the mess tent, and tossed it on the table like it was a sack of feed. They grunted loudly with the weight.

"Nothing weighs more than a corpse," said Barnett.

"That's because it's *dead* weight, dumb ass," growled Chavis.

I stared at Rawlings's frozen death smile in the lantern light and noticed the skin on the face glowed with a bluish tint. My father once told me a story about how the dairyman brought fresh milk to the house during the Great Depression in big metal cans.

My grandmother would carry out her pails and order two gallons of "blue john." The dairyman always ladled the cream off the top and poured the skimmed milk into her pails. Without the expensive yellow cream, what was left had a blue-gray color, and all the women around town called it blue john. Rawlings was missing the ingredient that gave him flavor, richness, taste, and vitality. He had become "blue Mike."

Johnson picked up the hand microphone for the PRC-25 and asked me, "How the fuck am I gonna call this in?"

"He got shot through the jugular vein. He was KIA, motherfucker, KIA," answered Barnett. "Oh, and by the way, Rawlings had a great collection of *Playboy* mags, which he'll no longer need. Dibs!"

"Then I'm calling dibs on the baseball cards and the pictures of his sister," yelled Johnson over the squawking radio.

Chavis stood and grinned. "Well, he's been hiding four cans of peaches that his mommy sent in her last care package and I'm *taking* those." He patted the grenade launcher riding on his hip. "Or else, whoever does better not sleep."

By that time, Wolfe's squad had crowded into the tent and everyone not on guard duty had joined in the argument over Rawlings's possessions. Sergeant Martin pulled me outside and I gave him a situation report as best as I could. Within a few minutes, things returned to business as usual inside the compound. After all, death was part of the business.

I understood the banter and the irreverence. Each one of those men respected Rawlings in their own way, and a piece of his property was a piece of Rawlings. Joking became the way to mourn without feeling guilty that you had survived. Besides, I dug out Rawlings's hidden bottle of Johnny Walker Red and drained it, toasting my friend and squad leader. The man had gotten his wish fulfilled in a different way, but Mike Rawlings flew home just like Willie Mason.

Late the next morning, a whole platoon of army soldiers came to collect the jeep. The lieutenant in charge bitched at Martin because there should have been a box of chocolate in the back seat that the driver had been bringing back from the Phu Bai PX. The army officer planned on mailing it to his wife for Valentine's Day and the candy had gone missing. I watched Martin's face turn purple as he fought to control himself and wondered if the lieutenant ever realized how close he came to having his head blown off.

Chapter 11

THE ROBIN

On January, 17, 1968, a strange blond man with dull blue eyes and thick, black-rimmed glasses stood beside me at the junction of Route 1 and a dirt path in our hamlet of Gia Le, Thua Thien Province, Republic of South Vietnam. We stood there because Nguyen Minh had just finished brewing a new batch of what he called wine. Actually, it was grain alcohol distilled from rice. After a few days of drinking it during my first week of CAG in early December, I quickly developed a calloused tongue and that allowed me to get the first shot down. Once the wine hit my stomach, it reminded me of Grandma McGarrah stoking the belly of her cast-iron stove with her right hand while holding me on her hip with the left. The flames licked upward from the black coal. The sparks flew from the tips of the fire and were belched out of a tin-throated pipe in the form of gray smoke. After that, a warm glow settled over the coal, the living room, and me. I was feeling that same glow on this particular morning after my third glass of Minh's pinkish liquid.

The blond man and I had stopped at Minh's makeshift bar on our way back to the compound. We were returning from the morning "medcap," which was a propaganda tool invented by some Marine Corps officer as part of pacification. Normally, one marine would provide armed escort for the navy corpsman, Rick Santos, but Santos had hitched a ride to Da Nang for supplies today. Our job was to hand out toothbrushes, toothpaste, soap, bandages, disinfectant, and antibiotics in his place. In return, we gathered military intelligence from the villagers in the marketplace and passed it on to Sergeant Martin, who filtered it and sent it forward to the Phu Bai command center. Since the Vietcong assassinated anyone who gave us correct information on their movements, our intelligence was usually worthless. But the officer in Phu Bai didn't know that, and I enjoyed helping any children who might happen to live past puberty keep their teeth with an unending supply of Crest. It blunted the edge of cynicism that had slowly replaced my youthful romanticism over the last few weeks. The Vietnamese had become human to me, and to participate in their suffering grew increasingly distasteful, especially as I read the news of mounting protests at home against the war, especially as I watched my friends die around me for no identifiable reason other than being in the wrong place at the wrong time. I had begun to concentrate on my own survival as the cause itself waned in my mind.

On our fourth drink, my partner, Lance Corporal Huffman, the blond man who had replaced Mike Rawlings, made an interesting observation.

"We haven't killed anyone this week."

"So?"

"So. This war's all about numbers. If we don't come up with a body count that makes the brass proud, they're gonna ship us back to our original units and we'll be out in the bush with the rest of the grunts. I don't know about you, but I like it here. It's easy to get killed, but at least there's a bar, whores, and a barber."

Huffman had a point. This war was about numbers, but military math was easily manipulated. This was another reason for my mounting distrust. If a hundred marines engaged a VC squad of ten and each force lost ten and two men respectively, then our casualties were 10 percent while enemy casualties were 20 percent. We won the battle. I realized that simple fact by reading the account of some operations and firefights that I had been on as the newspapers mom sent from home caught up with me. The communists suffered heavy losses in print while I carried my friends out of the jungle in body bags.

Thinking was beginning to give me a headache. Huffman yawned and stretched his arms toward the early morning sun. A black speck stuck in the corner of my right eye. I tried to wipe it away, quickly realizing it wasn't in my eye. The speck squatted in a rice paddy about a hundred meters from Minh's front porch.

"Look at Victor Charlie taking his morning potty break. He don't even know we're here," said Huffman. "What are you waiting for?"

"What do you mean?"

"This is a war, stupid. I'm standing here with a 12-gauge shotgun. I couldn't kill a fly at thirty yards. Shoot the son of a bitch before he wipes his ass and leaves."

He was right. The shot was mine. The boy had appeared from out of the background behind a cluster of small huts, like a weed in a garden. The garden needed pruning, and my M-16 was the right tool for the job. At least those were the kinds of stupid images I conjured up since this killing would be a process of consciousness. In a firefight, everything moved faster than thought. A firefight, no matter what size, was a reactionary reality. The instinct of survival pulled triggers, not me, not my mind. This morning the circumstance was different. I had time for thought. I had to will a young man dead who didn't even know I existed, whose only mistake as far as I could tell was dressing himself in a tattered black uniform, who some politician in a country ten thousand miles from here said was evil. Looking first at the boy, then at my rifle, I remembered being ten years old.

My father gave me a Daisy air rifle. The shiny copper BBs loaded into a long tube beneath the blue metal barrel. The rifle was a remarkable gift because it marked a change of direction in my life. I had acquired real power, no longer needing a cap pistol and an over-developed imagination. When I pointed my new toy at an object and pulled the trigger, damage was inflicted. I controlled the destiny of anything within a radius of thirty yards. Also, my father's willingness to trust me with such a weapon indicated that he viewed me as a child with gender—a man-child, almost ready to insure his immortality.

In the backyard of our home on West Broadway, an ancient walnut tree guarded the northwest corner. Pears dangled from limp limbs on another tree beside my bedroom window. Next to the garage, a crumbling chicken coop leaned toward the driveway. On the sill of its one broken window, coffee cans and Coke bottles perched openly, unaware of the danger lurking in the shadows of the back porch. My favorite target was a rusty fifty-five-gallon drum that my mother used as a trash incinerator. There were no laws in 1958 regarding refuse. Any person living in Princeton, Indiana, could burn a myriad of toxic materials with a clear conscience. The drum became an enemy soldier. It was just about my height, and the ashes inside made a neat thump when hit with a BB.

My skills became formidable. I rolled and fired through the heart of the barrel like Audie Murphy shooting cattle rustlers and bank robbers. Mom screamed, "Hey, what happened to my trash can? It looks like Swiss cheese. Go shoot something else." Striding forward forcefully, rifle at the hip, dropping one can after another as they peeked out of the chicken coop, I became John Wayne, struggling with wild Indians. But the problem with target practice is that it implies honing a skill for other uses. Targets don't move, breathe, challenge, or invoke adrenaline. Eventually, they generate only boredom. I needed to confront the reason that weapons exist. I needed to shed blood.

Staying in the shadow of the bar, I slid down quietly and stretched out in a prone position. The target was close, but lying flat on the dirt steadied my slightly trembling trigger hand. With this rifle I could hit a man's forehead at twice the distance. My right cheek rested wetly against the plastic rifle stock. Sweat dripped, one drop at a time, from my nose onto the bolt and over the selector switch, which was set on semiautomatic. One shot was all it would take. There was no use sacrificing accuracy just to hear a fully automatic burst of fire. I never understood why Americans were so in love with loud noises and explosions. Maybe it had something to do with Black Cat firecrackers, cherry bombs, the Fourth of July, the belief in cowboys and heroes; or maybe loud noises just drowned out the sound of our consciences.

A light mist rose like gauze curtains from the paddy water and parted gently around my target. I adjusted windage and elevation on the rifle sight carefully, though the breeze was mild. The smell of dead fish and rotting vegetation clung to the humidity and strangely I was comforted. The odor of death was also the odor of life. Every day, I consumed death just to survive—dead meat, dead plants. When I died, something would consume me and continue existence. It all seemed so natural. As I tightened my grip on the stock and slowly compressed the trigger, I prepared to swallow death one more time. But would I be nourished any more than I was on a particular Sunday in 1958?

While the rest of the family took a Welch's grape juice communion at the Broadway Christian Church, I faked a sore throat and sighted down my Daisy barrel. A robin flitted from a tree branch to a pile of fallen pears from the tree outside my bedroom window. Its red breast glittered with dew and sunlight. Air thumped as I squeezed the trigger. A shiny copper ball fled the barrel, like a falling star flees the sky. The robin danced. Its wings kept time with the fluttering of my heart. Its ruddy chest dampened with a dirty crimson. Watching this graceful minuet of death, I felt exhilarated, as if I had just hit a home run in a Little League game, or been kissed on the cheek by Denise Collins, my blue-eyed neighbor with developing breasts. When the bird fell over, frozen and breathless, my stomach seemed to rise into my mouth, like it did when Dad drove the car too fast over the top of Fischer's Hill. I wanted to take the moment of impact back. I wanted to shout at God and tell him that there had been a mistake. I was only playing. Instead I cried and buried the robin before my parents came home from church.

The bolt of my M-16 hit the primer. The casing spit lead down the barrel. The bolt ejected the casing and I heard a pop like a pricked party balloon. I was no longer in control of my enemy's destiny. The bullet was.

"You missed. How could you miss? You could've made that shot blindfolded in a fucking hurricane."

A soldier never hears the shot that kills him. The boy in the rice paddy heard the water splash, felt the wet spray, and was running, pants in hand, by the time the sound of exploding gunpowder reached him. My shot landed about a foot to the right of his squatting ass. I hit exactly what I intended to hit. I killed a lily pad. There was no use chasing him. He could have ducked into a tunnel entrance or into his cousin's living room by the time we reached the group of huts beyond the rice paddy. Huffman kicked dirt, pounded the bar top, and sputtered loudly.

"You asshole. You missed him on purpose, didn't you? Didn't you? Keep treating these animals like they're human and see if you don't end up dead, you silly fucker."

"I wasn't sure he was VC. Were you? He didn't even have a rifle."

"He was probably planting a booby trap in the paddy."

"Oh yeah. Where was he carrying it, up his ass? And why, so he could blow up some water?"

"He was a gook. Kill one now, it's one less we gotta kill later."

We bought a bottle of Minh's rice wine and continued the argument while walking back to the compound. The sun was white and hot. My head still hurt and my jungle fatigues were soaked with sweat. I wanted to tell Huffman the truth. Instead, we discussed the sanctity of human life, the nature of politicians, the heat, how to fry C ration bread, the best cigarettes, pound cake and peaches, the hope that this one boy who was allowed to live another day might have a good-looking sister.

I never told my Dad about the robin. Once he asked me, "What happened to your BB gun? I haven't seen you kill any cans lately." I just said, "It's in the closet." How could I say that I couldn't even bear to look at it? How could I tell a blond-haired, teenage killer, how could I tell myself that I hadn't gone completely over, that even with my idealistic notions shattered I still wanted to hope, that when I sighted a small, yellow boy, all I saw was a dead bird.

Chapter 12

THE SKY IS CRYING

Maybe no one really had "the luck." Maybe it passed through you like sunlight through a windowpane. You felt its warmth even though it had moved on. It couldn't be captured. It couldn't be held. Maybe what you kept close all the time was the hope that some special force unknown to everyone but you had trapped the luck inside you and you were shielded from the contagion of death that infected everything else.

As long as we all pretended to believe this nonsense individually, we could collectively function because each of us remained invincible in our minds. What would happen if we felt the luck leave? Rick Santos made me think about this for years after I left Vietnam.

* * *

Four days before the January 31, 1968, Tet Offensive, my squad was scheduled for night ambush. Since military intelligence had put several divisions of NVA moving through our TAOR, we had quit pushing our patrols out beyond the village perimeter, especially at night. The CAG was outgunned when it came to dealing with large forces of regular soldiers and not designed for large-scale infantry operations. So, night ambush usually meant nothing more than walking slowly to the playground of the old French schoolhouse, sitting in a tight semicircle with our backs against the schoolyard wall, where we waited for sunrise, hopefully undetected.

I never knew anymore when a platoon of enemy soldiers might end up in our collective lap. On this night, the possibility made me feel more twitchy than usual for some reason, as if I were a rabbit downwind of a dog. It might have been the amphetamines Santos passed out like M&Ms to keep us awake for days at a time. They had long since ceased generating any clarity of thought because my body and mind were exhausted. I was left with a kind of captured static electricity bouncing around inside my skull, shocking my nervous system into autonomic responses. My leg lifted and stepped forward, my arms raised and gripped the rifle, but all without purpose or understanding. I fought the paranoia induced by the chemical and the sense of impending doom that had choked me since Mike Rawlings died.

The squad set up around midnight. I placed Mac Barnett and the M-60 machine gun at the top of the semicircle. By taking the middle position, the gun could sweep a full thirty meters in either direction, giving it command of the full length of the killing zone. I loved the way the Marine Corps labeled things. The field of fire that offered the highest possibility of slaughtering an unsuspecting group of humans wasn't a back-shooting ambush, a butcher's block, blood alley, or carnage carnival. It was simply a zone, a technical term. Marines were expected to get in the zone and stay there as if they were swinging a hot bat in a high school baseball game.

Fanning to the left and right and slightly behind Barnett, Tri, Flea Chavis, and the other squad members slid down into prone firing positions, checked their weapons, and waited silently, hidden by the darkness and the tall elephant grass. Tugging at Ron Johnson's sleeve, I pulled him behind Barnett and sat him down. If we should get into a firefight and need to call for support, the radio would be located close by and protected. Sergeant Martin had given me the temporary job of squad leader. Although Lance Corporal Huffman had come out as Mike Rawlings's replacement, my three days' seniority as a lance corporal put me in this position of outranking him. I harbored no desire to be in charge but would fulfill the responsibility while Martin figured out a correct military solution to the dilemma. I may have been the only point man/squad leader in Marine Corps history.

Somewhere behind us all and in front of the schoolyard wall, Santos found a spot to wait with his morphine and pressure bandages ready.

The squad had decent cover. We would be unseen by any troops moving over the thin, dirt path directly in front of us. The tree line beyond the path was silent except for a few jungle birds cawing. The moon filtered a pale yellow glow through the clouds. I began to drift inside my mind while slumped over the rifle and lifted the hand mike off of the PRC-25 radio on Johnson's back. Pressing the transmit button twice would make the receiver in the compound click twice, and the rest of the unit would know the squad had set the ambush safely without making any sound on our end. I felt so exhausted that my body didn't want to stay awake even in the dangerous situation of an ambush. Thankfully, the pills kept me from completely drifting off.

I reflected on a filly, one whose racing career my father had followed religiously for the past two years. She was listed as a blood bay because all four legs were black above her ankles, but her sleek body shined a bright red color in the sun. A single white patch of hair grew between her eyes in the shape of a star. When I had seen this thoroughbred break from the starting gate, I had been amazed. She reached out and flowed over the track like a feral river flooding its banks with grace and natural efficiency. I believed my dad loved the horse because she ran every race with integrity, never spitting out the bit until the finish line had been crossed.

At the darkest hour right before dawn, I began to see her running along the tree line. The jockey rode low on her neck, pushing the reins up behind her ears. The rider had my father's face and clucked and drove her toward the wire. She was gaining on something . . . she was there . . . come on baby, run. "Cluck . . . cluck . . . cluckcluckcluck."

"Shit."

"What the fuck . . ."

"Damn, Santos, you almost blew my head off."

Barnett shouted and rolled away from his M-60 machine gun. I suddenly realized that the clucking noise was Santos's AK-47 spraying bullets into the shadows of a dying night. According to the Geneva Convention, navy corpsmen and army medics must not be armed. However, since the NVA refused to recognize that particular treaty, we all thought it best to give Santos a rifle. That way, the enemy didn't recognize him and focus on him as their first target to prevent him from treating others. I loaned him a weapon I had taken off the body of an NVA officer killed in a fierce firefight right after Christmas. I taught the healer how to use it and the healer learned reluctantly, always uncomfortable with the idea of actually having to use it.

The last time I'd seen Santos, he leaned against the low cement wall that surrounded the schoolyard. His eyes rolled back in his head and the AK-47 rested, like a limp dick, between his legs. Now, crawling toward the wall and the gunfire, I saw Santos kneeling beside a black lump. Johnson radioed for the mortar crew in the compound to fire flares while the squad held their positions.

"Shit. Oh shit. Mother of God." Santos rocked back and forth over the motionless lump.

A flare popped and its canister fell from the sky with a hollow whisper. I turned the shadow over. A thin, yellow boy stared unblinking into my face. The kid was thirteen, maybe fourteen, with greasy hair and a white scar above his left eye. In the fluorescent glow of the flare, the boy seemed part of the earth that had

Checking weapons during Tet 1968 siege of CAG unit.

broken off, without humanity, a surreal piece of loose soil. Maybe this is what the old timers meant by saying that the jungle grows when the ground gets irrigated with blood.

"You shot a VC. Where'd he come from?"

"I don't know. Swear to God, I don't know. He's just a baby."

"A baby that wanted to kill you."

I grabbed the boy's slack arms and rolled him right. Beneath the body, an old Thompson submachine gun lay in the grass, safety off and round chambered. If the kid had been a seasoned fighter with quicker reactions, Santos would have been the one we carried back in a rain poncho. Once more his luck had saved him.

"You're my hero," whispered Flea.

"No use whispering now. With all the noise we've made, most of I Corps knows where we are. I'd say it's time to move before his friends show up," Barnett suggested, and the suggestion was a wise one.

"The kid must have been sneaking along the schoolyard wall, trying to get into the marketplace . . ."

Johnson cut me off in mid sentence.

"Yeah, to plant a booby trap for one of us to trip on."

"The little sucker stumbled over Doc's big-ass feet and got himself blown away," Flea said. "Talk about some seriously bad mojo. Killed by a stinky-ass jungle boot and a sleeping corpsman."

"You only Boc-si ever kill Charlie in sleep," said Tri, who was now searching the boy's pockets for useful information.

"Shut up. How am I going to explain even having this gun?"

"Nobody has to know you shot him. When I report to the CO, I'll give kill credit to someone else." I looked around at the rest of the squad. "Who wants the kill?"

Flea waved. "Me. I already got eight confirmed. This one and another one and I'm off to Hong Kong for five days." He looked at the Vietnamese in the squad. "And I want you little fuckers to know that your ears are just as yellow as his."

No one argued because no one wanted to piss Flea off and then have to walk in front of him on patrol. The commander of the four CAG units had a deal with his marines. Any man who could confirm ten dead enemy soldiers by his own hand received five days of liberty anywhere in Southeast Asia, even if he'd already gone on R & R once. I hated the deal because farmers looked like Vietcong when they were dead. If a guy like Flea got close to ten, the temptation was often too great and some harmless old man or woman ended up dying, minus the ears. In my mind that was still murder and there were some lines I just simply refused to cross.

This kill was clean, though, and I never gave the boy's age a second thought. When a child shoots you in the heart, you're still dead. Only Santos seemed agitated by any form of moral dilemma. We threw the body onto a rain poncho, and then I made the Vietnamese drag it through the village at a fast pace. Back at the compound, Flea and Barnett hung it upside down on the concertina wire as a warning. The corpse would disappear before it rotted. Soon some local family member would sneak into the area late one night, pull it off the wire, and bury it. We would let it happen.

As the sun rose hot, Santos and I crawled into our bunker. Once Rawlings died, I had been invited to move into the bunker that he had shared with Santos and Flea. It was a move up in status and respect. I couldn't refuse. Besides, in the typical fast-forward intensity of combat, the navy corpsman and I had connected at some primal level that transcended ordinary friendship. We spoke the same slang, drank the same nasty whiskey, had the same taste in women, felt lied to and cheated by the U.S. government, couldn't wait to get back to college, and were bound by a thread of hope that our lives still had some purpose. The relationship was symbiotic. Santos counted on me to keep him alive physically and I counted on him to keep me alive emotionally. At least that's the way things were till he shot the kid by accident on night ambush.

Santos lit a Thai stick and we smoked lying on our cots.

"I can't sleep."

"Stop taking the speed you're supposed to give us."

"That's not it. I close my eyes, I see his face."

Santos stared at the ceiling motionless with his hands behind his head. He held his breath, forcing the smoke to saturate his lungs. I took a drag from the joint and followed his gaze upward, wondering what the corpsman was looking for.

"Whose face?"

"The kid's." Smoke exploded from Santos' lungs. "I close mine but his eyes are in my brain wide open, staring at me. What if he liked baseball? What if he had a baby sister that he was feeding, or an old crippled mama-san that couldn't get out of bed to pee without his help . . ."

Squirming, I sat up and passed him the joint.

"Listen to me . . . that little prick would have blown your brains out and probably nailed two or three more of us if he hadn't been unlucky enough to trip over your jungle boots in the dark. You still don't get it. You wear a peace sign on your helmet and you want to adopt every one of these little fuckers with a dirty face. I feel sorry for some of them too, but this is a war and they all hate us. Your DEROS is in six fucking days, man. You've been in this country over twelve months. Six more days and you're on the big bird back to the world. Wait till you get home, and then lead a goddamn march or something. By God, I'll join you in a few months."

"No, you don't get it." Santos' words slowed as the marijuana smoke laced with opium lifted his mind onto another plane and his eyes onto the shadows rustling in the candlelight across the uneven sandbag walls. "I'm in the navy, man. I'm in the fucking navy. I joined a pussy service so I wouldn't have to waste anybody in this war. I'm not a big bad killer like you guys."

"I bet you don't want to be killed either."

We both giggled, and then his face froze.

"Some things are worse than dying."

"You're stoned, man. Nothing's worse than dying because there's nothing after dying. You just get thrown in a big hole while someone shovels dirt on your unfeeling face, while some no-account bastard who never made it to 'Nam is screwing your girl because she needs comfort now that you're dead."

"It's all pretty simple to you, isn't it?"

"It's as basic as it gets. It's just like playing baseball in Princeton, Indiana. Win or lose. Kill or be killed." I lied to my friend. Vietnam had never been that simple.

Santos threw his legs up off the cot and stretched. The tin ceiling seemed to be getting closer and closer to my forehead.

"There's got to be more to it than that."

"Why?"

"Because humans can't fly."

Flapping his arms like wings, Santos jumped up from the cot and spun around the tight quarters twice. Then he fell backward laughing against a poster of Jimi Hendrix on the wall. The laughter evolved into a type of hysterical whine, like a tea kettle overheating.

"For Christ's sake, Santos, people die in your arms every day over here and you deal with it. Don't get so melodramatic."

"They die with me trying to save them. They don't die because I killed them. I can't explain it to you. There's something wrong with me. I don't feel right anymore. Oh my God . . ."

"What's wrong now?"

"What if I get home next week and strangle my sister or my mother in their sleep? What if I go crazy and can't control myself? I'm a killer."

"You're already crazy, and you're not going to kill anybody back home."

The fuel oil ran low in the smudge pot. The candle flames began to flicker. The bunker drifted into darkness. Meanwhile, the world outside kept getting brighter.

*   *   *

Wailing woke me. The noise was animal, but the source was human. Stumbling over Santos' empty cot, I threw the plastic sheet that served as a door aside and stepped into a white-hot sun. Through my confusion, I knew it must have still been morning because the scent of fresh coffee and fried bread mingled with the stench of urine. In country I learned to measure time by certain smells, by hunger, by an "X" on the calendar, or by the daily mail run from Phu Bai.

Several of the guys ran from the mess tent toward the sound. I checked the magazine on my M-16, chambered a round, and followed the crowd. Tri spoke in sharp, clipped words with an old man, his mouth pouring out the sounds so fast that I was lost. If I could have seen the sounds in print with the accent marks properly placed, then I might have recognized some of the words and made an effort at understanding the conversation. Even in my stupidity, it was easy to guess who they were talking about. A gnarled piece of flesh lay bundled in a plastic sheet. It looked like what was left of a woman, probably around sixty years old. A makeshift tourniquet knotted around her left thigh kept jerking in time with the twitching muscle. Below it, a mangled mess of flesh and bone dangled by a sliver of ligament.

The old man, who seemed to be her husband, shook a big shell casing in Tri's face with both hands. A young woman was the source of the wailing. She held three dirty, sobbing children close. Santos knelt over the body and shut the woman's eyes with the palm of his hand. He looked at Tri, then the old man. His face was the color of white birch bark and his pudgy cheeks rose and fell rapidly as he panted like a dog. The canister had come from an American mortar shell.

"Tell him his wife's already dead. The twitching is involuntary. There's nothing I can do."

"What happened here?" I asked.

"When we called for flares last night, this canister fell away from one and went through their roof. It sliced the old woman's leg off while she was sleeping. She must have died of shock as they carried her here."

"Jesus."

"Jesus didn't have a thing to do with this classic fuck up," said Sergeant Martin, who had arrived behind me. "Somebody will want to get even, so keep your eyes open."

Tri stepped back and handed me the canister. The old man mumbled, the woman wailed, the children continued sobbing.

"He say you pay for wife. Beaucoup piasters. You kill, you pay."

"Tell him it was an accident. Please accept the apology of the United States government." Martin nodded at the old man, dismissing him with a wave of his hand.

After Tri turned and shouted a few phrases into the old man's ear, the family attached themselves to the plastic sheet and pulled the body back down Route 1, as if they were returning from the market with a load of groceries.

"What did the guy say?" I asked Tri.

"He say no such thing as accident in war."

Santos seemed to clutch his stomach at Tri's words and rose slowly. He lost his balance every couple of steps walking back to the bunker.

"Now what?" I yelled at the back of Santos' head.

"Now I smoke a bowl of opium."

"Hey, not without me," shouted Barnett.

"Or me, white boy," Flea said, from the corner of the guard shack.

I watched the three of them disappear into our bunker. The rest of the crowd split away in different directions, some to write letters, some to clean weapons, some to mount the morning patrol. I was left alone to contemplate the lack of discrimination death always showed in Vietnam, and how it became part of the normalcy of life, like cooking, sewing, eating, and pissing. Each of us suffers alone while the rest of the world enjoys dinner. Rather than think too long, I sought comfort in what was available to create a distraction and found myself at Co Le Ly Diem's front door.

Diem was a beautiful woman. Her father had been a French paratrooper, or French priest. I never got the story straight and she probably didn't care. When the French were thrown out in the early 1950s, the girl's mother raised her daughter to take over the family business as part of the great Vietnamese civilian contingent that serviced the military complex on either or both sides. It was a good living, Diem had told me, especially after the Americans brought beaucoup penicillin into the village. I always purchased her services without guilt and today felt willing to pay an extra ten dollars worth of military script for her to whisper "Katie" in my ear. I knew the danger of being alone in the village had increased after the last night's activities, but I didn't really give a damn. I needed to touch something soft, something that wasn't metal, something warm.

The sun hung directly overhead and was very hot when I left Diem's bedroom and walked the few yards through the concertina wire into camp. The men who weren't on day patrol slept in the cool air of their sandbagged bunkers. Freddie Thomas sat behind the M-60 machine gun at the gate half-dozing, and waved me in. I waved back, as if Thomas was a crossing guard and I was on the way to school. The quiet morning gave me a strange feeling of security. Everything seemed okay and the day in Vietnam became the same as the day everywhere else. I wanted to go help my friend Santos pack for the trip home, to tell him thanks for being there with a listening ear after Rawlings's death. I wanted to be concerned for Santos the way I knew the corpsman was for me and everyone else in the CAG.

Santos sat outside their bunker on an old ammo box with his back to the camp, staring across the rice paddies and into the trees. Nothing moved, not even the air around me as I walked. There were no cries, squawks, squeals, or chirps. Reaching out to tap Santos on the shoulder gently, so as not to startle the man, I imagined what his thoughts might be—pale women, the secret ingredients of Twinkies, playing softball with a fraternity team, med school, going home. It was all about going home. Nothing else mattered in Vietnam, just going home.

The air filled with the smell of gunpowder, the sound of a small firecracker exploding under a coffee can, and the texture of wet sand simultaneously. "SNIPER!" I screamed while my friend slumped over the rifle that rested between his knees. Diving into the trench directly in front of Santos, I waited for another round to be fired. The world remained silent. Santos slid off the ammo box sideways and fell beside me. I stared into the vacuum of his open eyes. I saw the tiny entry wound on the point of his chin and for a split second felt the bullet rip upward through the roof of my own mouth, tear through the sinus cavities and the frontal lobe of the brain, and finally, explode out the top of my skull. I felt no pain, just curiosity. There were immediate questions about the angle of entry. There were other questions, but I couldn't ask myself those. I began picking up gray matter and pieces of skull from the floor of the trench, packing them back into the cavity as if I might somehow reanimate his body before the others arrived.

"SNIPER. GET THE FUCK DOWN!"

Flea and Barnett rushed around the corner of the bunker. They dove into the trench and came up, weapons pointed into the silent tree line. Martin stood behind us all and yelled.

"There's nothing there. The shot must have come from the temple."

Martin pointed and we all three turned toward the temple that rested behind us in the center of our compound. It was the village landmark and sacred. The doors were all padlocked to remind us not to enter and loot the place for souvenirs. The CAG had followed orders and camped around it because Howdy Doody believed it would be the safest place. The VC would not want to create a public relations nightmare by destroying the temple. It was a weak theory, but we did as we were told.

Now, Martin seemed convinced that a sniper had somehow tunneled into the temple through the floor and singled out Santos for assassination because of the goodwill he created in the village with his med-cap patrols. We kicked the temple door in and found the interior empty. Without checking further, I brought Martin a satchel charge and he blew the building to pieces. Standing in the midst of the smoking rubble, I watched Tri, Phuc Tran, and the rest of the Popular Forces troops hang their heads in shame. All I felt was anger.

I could never actually form the words in my conscious mind

to question how Santos had been shot in the front of his head from behind, or how the bullet had traveled vertically instead of horizontally. I accepted the theory of a lone gunman in the temple window for the same reason the public had accepted the lame version of President John F. Kennedy's death, because it was easiest. All I knew for sure was from that moment forward, nothing seemed exactly right in my mind. It was like I walked around with my head cocked sideways and took the world in from the wrong angle. I built an elaborate system of answers to the questions I was afraid to ask. Slowly in my memory, I gave the sniper a face, a rifle, a family, even a name. I cursed that nebulous thing called luck because my friend's ran out and it wasn't right that it happened the way it did. I felt the luck flow into me as it poured from Santos, a gift I hadn't asked for. That first night after the death when the thoughts came, the ones beyond instinct, the ones that reflected events clearly like photographs, I wanted to somehow exorcise the luck. I finally understood why my friend hated it. No one could carry it without carrying the guilt that went with it.

In the darkness of the bunker every night after Rick Santos died, I couldn't stop going back to the silence before the gunshot and the stunning silence that remained after. Something was hiding in that space between the two silences, and it was like a lit fuse. It had to be discovered to be extinguished, but I had no desire to see where it led.

Chapter 13

CAHN CHO

On January 31, the morning that the 1968 Tet Offensive really began and a few hours before the Vietnamese militia left our compound and went home, I was invited to breakfast by Tri. It was quite an honor. We were under siege conditions and on twenty-four-hour alert. Even though the Vietcong and a platoon of North Vietnamese regulars had remained practically invisible in the days following Rick Santos's death, we could feel their presence. They had created a gauntlet for us to walk through if we dared leave the compound. It was similar to being back in America driving drunk in a dense fog and anticipating that a semitruck had drifted into the wrong lane and was bearing down on you around the next curve. The difference was that back home, I knew the fog would lift and the road would straighten. For the last several days, Vietnam had been all curve and all fog and the expectation terrified me. Contact would have been a relief.

An occasional sniper fired into the latrines or at the watchtower during the daylight hours, and at night sappers probed the concertina wire, keeping us awake and tormenting us with the constant possibility of being overrun.

Logic told us we weren't worth the risk. We had been in this place for several months, some of the unit longer than others. Other than well-armed men, a small group of stray puppies hardened and made thin by the struggle to survive, some rats, and an occasional snake, nothing of intrinsic value to either side in this war existed within our camp. The ambushes and firefights we participated in had made us a tough and competent bunch of teenage boys. The village we protected was poor and contained very little in the way of material goods that the VC could use. Why would they invite heavy casualties simply to kill a few American marines and Vietnamese peasants? We knew they were more interested in the imperial city of Hue, a little more than a mile north.

Nevertheless, our collective logic had been suspended by the emotions of war. The sniping and probing kept our imaginations working overtime. On top of that, the VC had set up an old public address system somewhere in the hills above the village, and in the darkness they called out our names in English, along with a bounty. It was an eerie feeling for me to know that I had a price on my head like a horse thief in cowboy country. As a point scout and tunnel rat I was worth about four American dollars in piasters, a large sum for a rice farmer earning the equivalent of twenty dollars a year.

Communications with headquarters in Phu Bai were limited. None of us knew that in the last few hours the whole country had been devastated by a surprise attack that violated the traditional Tet cease-fire, or that the American embassy in Saigon had been overrun. I had no idea that this invitation to breakfast was the way the Vietnamese troops who lived within our compound had chosen to say goodbye. I felt good about being asked to join them in their inner sanctum, a small cluster of sandbagged bunkers on the northeast side of the camp. This was their private lair and the celebratory meal for the lunar New Year. After weeks of cold C rations, a bowl of piping hot stew with fresh meat and slightly wilted vegetables seemed too good to pass up.

I had no misconceptions about why the invitation had been offered to me and not the rest of my squad. At the time, I was a small, wiry, deeply tanned young man, and when I spoke with the Vietnamese it was eye to eye. I didn't tower over them like the rest of my squad. I didn't intimidate them with my size or arrogance and I made every effort to understand them on their terms. No, I couldn't speak the language well, but through a combination of charades, broken French, and pidgin Vietnamese, we were able to pass messages back and forth with uncommon alacrity and accuracy.

"Chow an, mayn yoi com?"

"You beaucoup dinky-dow Jeemy. Eat now," said Tri as he made shoveling motions toward his mouth with an imaginary fork.

I treated them with as much respect as I could muster, considering it was impossible to tell who sold information to the VC for extra cash. This was their country, not mine. I saw them as humans, not slopes, gooks, or zipperheads, but individuals with unique personalities who found themselves caught and confused between terrorists from their own country and terrorists from the United States who were called Americans but spoke English. I didn't trust them when it came to choosing between my life and theirs, but I liked them. They were intelligent and had a gentle resignation that resided in their deep-set black eyes. This was especially true of Tri. He and I had walked point together so many times we seemed like conjoined twins. I knew what his next step would be before he took it. He knew what my next order would be before I gave it. If I had felt able to trust any of them, it would have been Tri. He hated the VC. They had murdered his uncle, a district elder, and left his aunt to grow rice alone.

Tri kept grinning and pulling me toward the warm smell of ginger, nuoc mam, and charbroiled meat.

"You likey cahn cho. Cahn cho beaucoup tasty. Voudrais-vous eat beaucoup? Di di mao. Beaucoup good."

"Maybe. Maybe not," I lied. Of course I would love a hot meal, especially one that smelled like barbecued ribs.

The cook fire was located on the concrete pad at the entrance to the ruins of the Buddhist temple we had just destroyed. The Popular Forces had built their bunkers around the temple as if the proximity to some god might shield them from the winds of lead and fire that could decimate the rest of us at any given moment. Now, like hope, even that symbol of infinity had been reduced to finite rubble.

An iron pot hung on a tripod above the fire and pale blue smoke seeped from under the lid. Five, maybe six Vietnamese men in their midtwenties sat around the fire with wooden bowls. Some extracted pieces of fresh vegetables and meat with chopsticks. Some wiped the bowls clean with C ration bread. All of them smiled at me, greasy chins shining in the dawn light. A boy named Phuc Tran nodded, slid sideways, and patted the vacated cement. A spot had been reserved for the *dien cai dao* (crazy) foreigner.

I surveyed the rice paddies outside the perimeter of our compound and marveled at how quiet the paddies and the jungle beyond them were. The paddies were empty, an unusual occurrence for this time of the morning. If no one was working the small green shoots in the brackish, ankle-deep water, some old Ba should have been taking a morning shit and fertilizing the ground. No metallic trill from the toucans or chatter from the monkeys lifted out of the tree line. The silence wasn't empty; it was the kind of quiet generated by an unseen power and the incredible fear of it, like the calm in the eye of a hurricane or the mute stares of my mother when my father came home drunk.

These were signs I might have noticed at the time had I not been so hungry for hot food and dazed by the quiet.

Phuc Tran dipped stew from the iron pot, first a bowl to me as honored guest and then a bowl to Tri as his commander. I nodded toward both men and began to shovel the vegetables and chunks of meat into my mouth with chopsticks. The larger pieces of food proved manageable for someone as clumsy as I was with the delicate utensils, but the rice was another story. Struggling like a baby in boxing gloves, I worked some grains up the side of the bowl and to the edge where I was able to push them into my mouth. Phuc Tran, Tri, and the other men around the fire giggled like schoolchildren. I could have been offended, I guess, but the childish pleasure in their laughter made me happy as well.

I have never in my life since that day eaten any cooked concoction that tasted better. The meat fell apart in my mouth and disappeared, almost like cotton candy. The leeks, water chestnuts, yams, bamboo sprouts, garlic, and carrots were so fresh that each one had its own significant burst of flavor, even in the heavy sauce. While eating the second bowl and hoping there would be enough left for the third, I happened to raise my head, noticing that even inside the compound wire it seemed unusually still. Where were the six yelping puppies that had been foraging in the trash bin the day before?

"Ou est di di mao le chien?" I asked Tri where the dogs had gone because I'd had my eye on one little scruffy pup with a dirty white coat that yelped playfully and swatted at flies with his right front paw like our family dog, Lance, did back in "the world." I felt lonely sometimes, and even though getting attached to any living thing in Vietnam was a dangerous idea, I had visions of making this pup my special pet. Alienated in a country that had no horses, oak trees, blue jays, or even a McDonald's, I looked constantly for some connection with home that could keep me from losing every vestige of humanity I thought I had retained. The half-starved pup gave me a sense of optimism. Somehow in the midst of this violent insanity, man's best friend could provide a tangible salvation that no god had even attempted.

"Cahn cho, cahn cho. You be dinky dow," said Tri, giggling and rubbing his bloated belly with large sweeping motions.

Events happen in war that the mind will not acknowledge at the time, sometimes not until years later, sometimes never. I wished later that this celebratory breakfast could have been one of those events. It wasn't. I assumed that Tri had no interest in stray dogs and just wanted me to enjoy the food. After my third bowl, I rose, wiped my chin, patted my belly, and walked back across Route 1 to the American side of our compound. Slinging my M-16 over my shoulder, I ducked into the communications bunker where Sergeant Martin and Bob Wolfe smoked Pall Malls and listened intently to the static on the PRC-25 radio.

"Where you been, boy?" asked Martin, whose tour of duty was in its final weeks.

"Tri invited me to breakfast."

"Who'd you eat?" Wolfe snarled. He smiled and squeezed the fire off the butt of his cigarette with a thumb and forefinger as his dead eyes stared through some hole in the universe over my shoulder. I guess he thought appearing oblivious to pain commanded respect among those of us who had been in country a shorter period of time. The truth of the matter was, I thought Wolfe to be a psychopath. He exhibited most of the symptoms I had learned from my one semester of intro to psychology and he seemed to really get off on killing anything and everything he could. In all the years since I returned from 'Nam, anyone who looks at me with a hollow stare like Wolfe's gets immediately added to my mental list of the deranged.

"The boys cooked something called cahn cho. Pretty tasty, I might add."

Martin laughed out loud and Wolfe shook his head in disgust.

"Dog stew. That's dog stew, you idiot. Haven't you noticed all the puppies hanging around the trash have gone missing?" said Martin. "I told you when you got here two months ago not to make friends with those chickenshit bastards, or eat the garbage they offered you."

My initial reaction was nausea, the kind of gut feeling you'd expect from a red-blooded American boy. What kind of people would slit the throats of little puppies, hold them by their back legs while they bled out, skin them, and then stew them like chickens over an open fire? I thought of the white pup, the one that had nuzzled my leg the night before begging for scraps of anything just to keep from starving, hanging on to life by the sheer strength of its will to survive. Enraged, I grabbed my M-16 and rushed out of the communications bunker, followed by the raucous laughter of my two fellow white soldiers.

Initially, I was unsure as to what my action might be. I felt angry enough to flip the selector switch on my rifle to full automatic and wipe out their whole unit. Fuck these heathens and their stupid war. Fuck my own stupidity for being here among them this long and not knowing what they ate. I thought about playing shortstop on my college team, fishing with my Uncle Jim, rolling around in the backseat of my 1957 Chevy Bel Air with Katie, boosting a case of Falls City beer off the Humphreys' back porch, and just cruising around Princeton, Indiana, on a summer night so clear I could see through the stars. I thought about how my father had vowed not to take a drink until I returned home safely, and how my mother was terrified every time she turned on the six o'clock news and listened to Walter Cronkite explain why the casualties were mounting. All of these things and several others ratcheted my mind into a frenzy of loathing and fear. I wanted to kill someone, anyone with yellow skin and the inability to play baseball.

By the time I crossed the road, my mind began returning to me. I slung the rifle and sucked in a huge lungful of air. Rounding the one standing wall of the temple, I looked for Tri. He had to be told that killing and eating defenseless animals was a sin. Silence shrouded me. I smelled the remaining wisps of wood smoke, the sour water and mud from the paddies, the constant curtain of gun oil that hung around any fighting unit, and the acidic fog rising from the piss tubes. Even fear, which always stank like decayed earth and rotted wood, drifted across the compound with the smoke. What I didn't smell, see, or hear were any Vietnamese soldiers. Their side of camp was completely deserted. I had no idea how they slipped out past the sentries posted at the gates on the north and south ends of Route 1, but they did. It was as if they knew that the battle for Hue had begun in earnest. Probably they did, informed by some cousin or nephew in the Vietcong. In the distance, the sounds of small arms, rocket-propelled grenades, claymore mines, mortars, and .50 caliber machine guns rose from the smoking Citadel.

* * *

For two more weeks, we waited to die. I fought sleep every night as we manned the trenches dug around the compound just inside the barbed wire. The new navy corpsman handed out amphetamines. Each night, the C-130 we called "Puff the Magic Dragon" breathed fire in the sky over Hue. The electric cannons and machine guns shot downward so fast that, even though only every fifth round was a tracer, red laserlike lines extended from the firing ports of the plane to the ground. Huey gunships whirred like angry hornets over our heads, flying back and forth from Phu Bai to the Citadel unleashing their rockets, stinging the ancient buildings across the Perfume River.

At dawn on most days, trucks came south through our compound carrying the wounded and the dead piled on their flatbeds like crimson sandbags. Still, we remained on twenty-four-hour alert and not one enemy soldier charged the wire. We had no idea where the NVA platoon waited in hiding. Sergeant Martin halted all patrols of any kind for any reason after Wolfe took a round through the chest and died during a routine trip to the marketplace.

My insides wound tighter and tighter, and I felt as if I might break like the mainspring on a cheap watch. I was too scared to smoke any more dope or drink the rice wine left behind by our vanishing allies. If death was coming for me, through the claymore mines, the tangled barbed wire, the hail of lead—if death wanted me that badly, then the least I could do was meet him head on and alert, like a man. I had learned that melodramatic ideal by watching John Wayne in *The Sands of Iwo Jima*. It never occurred to me there in the jungles of Southeast Asia to remember that, after his death and the cameras shut down, Wayne rose from the grave to be killed several more times by redskins, outlaws, and other unnamed enemies of America.

To pass the time and keep my head from exploding, I manned roadblocks just outside the front gate twice as often as I was assigned to. Route 1 was crammed with refugees fleeing south, away from the battle for Hue. Each man, woman, and child had to be patted down and searched for weapons and booby traps. Captain Howdy Doody gave us that order direct from headquarters. Guessing he didn't want any VC sneaking into his concrete bunker in Phu Bai disguised as a houseboy or his favorite whore, I read identification cards for Howdy and checked the pictures on them to make sure the faces matched. Tri and the rest of the militia remained invisible and in their homes, as far away from our compound as possible.

Somewhere toward the end of the second week, I noticed that the string of refugees was braided with several young men. This seemed unusual to me since all the young men I had come in contact with previously were either in the South Vietnamese army or were VC. I pulled them out of line. Reading their ID cards, I noticed an odd stamp from the University of Hue. After many arm-flailing charades and the piecing together of slang from three different languages, I realized that what I held in my hand were student draft deferments. These bastards ate little puppy dogs and got out of military service by going to college. The irony wasn't lost on me and I grew overwhelmed with rage, as I seemed to do more easily and often on these days of silence and waiting.

By the time we changed the guard at dusk and I walked back to my bunker, a hatred so large that it choked all vestiges of humanity grew within me. Grabbing the M-79 grenade launcher away from my last remaining bunkmate Flea, I broke it open and loaded a white phosphorus round in the chamber.

"Where you going with my baby and that willie peter round?" shouted Flea at the back of my head.

Without answering, I lobbed the shell straight into the village. The explosion was beautiful. Normally, it would have been against the rules of engagement to take a shot like that in an area populated by civilians, but since the Tet Offensive, and given our location in the middle of an NVA troop route, the village had been declared a free-fire zone. All I had to say was that I saw movement after curfew, so I said it.

When white phosphorus, nicknamed willie peter, explodes, pieces of the chemical fly upward and then drift back to earth like fiery snowflakes. The flakes stick to whatever they touch. On contact with skin, the sparks burrow into flesh burning as they go. Most of the men I knew who had experienced willie peter wounds said they would rather have stood in the middle of a swarm of angry bees until stung to death. That, they agreed, wouldn't have been as painful.

Aimed by anger and fired at random, my round struck the front porch of the village barbershop. Within seconds the thatch walls blazed, and within minutes they collapsed. Villagers from neighboring homes doused their property with buckets of well water and escaped any ancillary fires. Since the shop had been closed and empty for days, I felt no guilt, and the catharsis of firing a weapon at anything calmed my nerves. I set about eating some pound cake and peaches left over from the day's allotment of C rations and watched Flea smoke a Thai stick.

* * *

Early in the third week of February, the Vietnamese militiamen straggled back into camp. Tri and Phuc Tran came first. None of them offered any explanation for their disappearance, and I was too exhausted from days of being on constant alert to chastise them about eating dog. Our squad of marines began to relax. We all figured that their return indicated the possibility of being attacked and overrun had been substantially reduced. I began to wander through the village again on my own at various intervals during the day, stopping to visit with the old women and bring Crest toothpaste to the children. Everyone tried sleeping cautiously.

On February 17 three mortar shells fell into the center of the compound. After the shelling, I found Phuc Tran lying on his back close to the standing south wall of the temple. There were no wounds on his chest, face, or arms, but he was dead. Tri came out of his bunker, followed by several others. Flea joined me and we rolled the boy over. His back fell away from his shoulders to his waist as if a giant meat cleaver had sliced it open. His smoking organs fell out onto the ground.

The next morning, we received orders from Phu Bai to send a patrol out through the marketplace to the north end of the village and clear a roadblock off Route 1. The trucks of wounded were already rolling from Hue. Tri and I led the squad out, and when we got to the brush, concrete blocks, and barrels, a force of about seventy-five NVA regulars caught us in a fierce crossfire. We had found them at last. The first burst of fire came from an AK-47 on full automatic. It must have been a very young soldier firing because the rounds zipped by my right ear and the ones that followed continued rising, as if the rifle had gotten away from the shooter's control. As I dove to the ground and rolled into a small culvert, an RPG round exploded on the cement road and lifted me up. I felt my flesh ripping, smelled it burning, and heard several dull thuds like someone had punched a canvas bag. The pain came much later, after the adrenalin quit churning in my veins.

The firefight lasted fourteen minutes. I also learned this fact later. It seemed hours at the time. The dead and wounded from both sides lined the road. Tri caught a bullet in the chest and died in a ditch on the opposite side of the culvert. I never had time to explain to him that eating dogs was savage. I was hit with shrapnel in several places along my left side and appeared to have a bullet hole in my foot, although I had no idea how it got there unless by some lucky shot when my body was in the air from the explosion. The roadblock was cleared.

Corporal Marty Smith saved my life by carrying me across his shoulders back to the compound. The navy corpsman stopped the bleeding with pressure bandages and I was laid on one of the trucks, along with a dozen other marines, some dead, some moaning, and some screaming as the truck careened from pothole to pothole on the shell-shocked highway.

The surgical tent in Phu Bai nearly burst at the seams with wounded, but after triage my turn to go under the knife came. Anesthetized by a confused-looking doctor in his late twenties, I don't know how much time elapsed before I began to wake up. The recovery room was tiled with stretchers so close together that the corpsmen barely had room to walk between them and to change the IV bottles dripping overhead. A few severely wounded Vietnamese civilians lay scattered among us marines. Although an unusual occurrence, I learned later that there was no room for them anywhere else and the doctors were trying to stabilize some of them enough to send them to makeshift Red Cross hospitals in the refugee camps. Some of the women and children had been there for days.

As my head cleared from the anesthesia, the people in the room came into focus, along with the white-hot pain in my body. No longer vague outlines of humanity, the details of their faces began to register. A small Vietnamese boy, maybe ten years old at the most, stared at me from the cot on my left. He seemed to know me and I began to realize that I knew him as well. I had seen him several times in the village playing on the floor of the barbershop while I got my hair cut. His entire body, except his face and arms, was wrapped in gauze. Two IV bottles dripped into his veins, and each time he tried to move his face warped into a repulsive grimace of pain. Closely patterned across the exposed flesh on his arms and face, small purple and black holes erupted that reminded me of an acne outbreak gone horribly bad. I recognized them as white phosphorus burns.

"How long's that kid been here?" I asked the corpsman when he came around to give me a morphine shot.

"A few days," he said. "That's a sad case of an innocent kid being in the wrong place at the wrong time. He's from a little village close to Hue. Best I can tell, he was playing in his father's shop when a random willie peter round went off on the front porch. Hell, this kid's burned so bad under those bandages that even if he lives, and that's unlikely, he'll be a fucking disfigured mess."

A bit groggy from the morphine, I heard the click of metal on metal as an IV bottle got hung somewhere in the room and the distant thump of an artillery battery as the outgoing shells flew toward Hue. A fuzzy image of me loading Flea's grenade launcher and firing the white phosphorus slowly seeped into my conscious mind.

"Is there anything you can do for him?"

"Best thing now would be a bullet in the brain."

Like most human beings who believe we're supposed to have consciences, I'd like to say that at this point I felt great remorse, was flooded with sadness, that the weight of what I'd done fell through my body and pulled me into the earth, burying me in shame. I'd like to say that, but the truth is I can't. I told myself that the boy had been injured by someone else, and I had no proof either way. I felt nothing but a slight disgust for this boy's parents, my emotions numbed by war and the novocaine of denial.

"What the fuck was he doing playing away from his parents? They ought to be horsewhipped. It's a war, for God's sake."

"He's a kid."

* * *

Many of my fellow marines considered me lucky, and I guess I was. I received the "million dollar wound," severe enough to finish my tour of duty in various hospitals, but not severe enough to leave me permanently disfigured or disabled. Still, not all disfiguring

MR. & MRS. JOHN W. MCGARRAH, BOX 282, OLD PETERSBURG ROAD, PRINCETON,
INDIANA. I DEEPLY REGRET TO INFORM YOU THAT YOUR SON LANCE CORPORAL
JAMES E. MCGARRAH 2371586 USMC, 3RD CAG, 3RD MAF, WAS INJURED ON 18
FEBRUARY 1968 IN THE VICINITY OF THUA THIEN, REPUBLIC OF VIETNAM. HE
SUSTAINED FRAGMENTATION WOUNDS TO THE LEFT FOOT AND LEFT LEG AS A
RESULT OF EXPLOSIVE DEVICE WHILE ENGAGED IN ACTION AGAINST HOSTILE
FORCES. HE IS PRESENTLY RECEIVING TREATMENT AT THE 3RD MEDICAL
BATTALION. HIS CONDITION AND PROGNOSIS ARE GOOD. YOUR ANXIETY IS
REALIZED AND YOU ARE ASSURED THAT HE IS RECEIVING THE BEST OF CARE.

ROBERT C. HALL
Major, U. S. Marine Corps
Inspector-Instructor
17th Rifle Company, FMF, USMCR
Evansville, Indiana 47712

Transcript of a radio message after being wounded.

wounds are noticeable to the public. That's the thing about combat on the ground and in your face. You always carry scars away from the battle, even if you don't bleed. I never knew if the barber's kid lived or died in that hospital ward. I never knew for sure that I injured him. But I've carried him around inside me for more than thirty years. His presence late at night has long overwhelmed the faces of enemies I killed and friends I watched die. The longer I live, the less comfortably I sleep, and the more I dream about the jungle. I see the boy sitting on the dirt floor of his father's barbershop playing some mindless game, laughing as the shell explodes, showering him with the innocuous-looking white flakes and then suddenly burning away his childhood. I imagine his father sobbing, wondering what horrible sin he'd committed to anger a vengeful American god and realizing, in confusion, his only offense was cutting hair.

Chapter 14

A GHOST IN THE MACHINE

The voice echoed in my ears for several minutes before I realized it was my own, and even then, I wasn't sure where it came from. It sounded like a normal voice, the kind of voice that spoke in a retail store when looking for a Christmas present for my mother, or the voice I might use to ask for another drink before the bar closed. It seemed to originate outside my head, though my own lips moved. It was that tone in the voice, the normal one, which made me think the sound came from somewhere else. How could I speak in such a way when my life had gotten so fucked up?

"This isn't the way I pictured visiting Japan."

I reached my right arm over my body to a small table on the left that separated the bed and another one just like it. Grabbing a pack of Winston cigarettes, I flicked aside a pen and a pad of paper with two fingers and found the lucky Zippo. Rolling over to retrieve the cigarette lighter, hot flames shot through my whole left leg and lit my brain on fire, forcing the voice back inside me and back out again. This time the tone was not so normal. "Jesus Christ that hurts. This *sure* isn't the way I pictured visiting Japan."

The man in the identical bed laughed loudly and spoke.

"I know what you're saying, man. I told the nurse yesterday that I still had at least two legs the same length and she could ride the middle one anytime. She said for me to shut up or she'd stuff a catheter in the one where my brains were. Nobody has any fun around here. When'd you get here from in country?"

"This morning. You were sleeping like a baby. They loaded my stretcher on a C-130 at Cam Rahn Bay and flew me straight to Tokyo, and then gave me a bumpy-ass ambulance ride from the airfield to the hospital. It took so long I pissed on myself. It's impossible to hit one of those chrome cups with the crooked necks when you're bouncing up and down on your back, so I held it as long as I could and then just let it fly."

"Gimme a smoke, will you?"

I shook a cigarette from the pack with one arm, picked it up and tossed it over.

"My name's Jim, Jim McGarrah."

The other man put the cigarette between his lips without lighting it. He stared at the ceiling as if trying to remember his own name.

"Glad to meet you, Jim. You can call me Nick. I must have been asleep when they brought you in."

"That's what I just said. You were snoring."

For the first time, I noticed the emptiness in Nick's bed just below the middle of his right thigh. The flat sheet ran from there to the end of the bed where it tucked neatly under the mattress. There wasn't a single wrinkle.

"You talk with a nasal twang," said Nick, and then picked up a straightened coat hanger. He leaned forward and reached with the coat hanger, using it to scratch a spot near the end of the bed where his foot should have been. "My toes itch."

"You don't have any."

"I know. It's a bitch. Where you from?"

Where was I from? A short time ago leeches fed on my blood. Snakes and rock apes and elephant grass surrounded me. People tried to kill me, the same people who had been trying for months, and they almost succeeded. Now I found myself in a white room, partially covered with white bandages and white sheets and lying next to a disheveled man whose eyes were glazed over with a ceramic boredom and who kept trying to scratch toes that didn't exist. In the center of the room, strapped to a metal support beam, hung a black-and-white television. *Bonanza* was playing and Hoss was talking to Little Joe. I tried to hear what was being said just to reorient myself with something familiar. "*Dozo irrishai mase.*" It didn't work as Little Joe answered, "*Domo arigato gozaimashita, Hoss.*" Where was I from?

"I'm from a little town in Indiana called Princeton. I can't wait to get back there and do something useful with my life."

"Yeah, it's good to be useful," said Nick.

How many summers had gone by since I rode my Schwinn bicycle from the west side of Broadway through the town square, pedaling hard past the courthouse, turning south on Main? How many summers had passed since I leaned that bike against the wood frame of Conway's Market and snuck in to buy an all-day Holloway Sucker with the milk money my mother had given me? It was a game we used to play. When I'd ride back home, she'd demand that milk. I'd say I forgot it. She'd send me back, where I'd exchange the sucker for the milk. That way I got plenty of exercise and, if there happened to be extra change in the household budget, she'd give it to me, saying, "Buy yourself a Holloway Sucker while you're there."

"Gimme another cigarette, will ya?" asked Nick and I was glad. I didn't want to think anymore about home. It would look the same as the day I left over a year ago, but it would never be the same place because I wasn't the same person.

"I'm so bored I feel like sticking my finger up my ass and then smelling it." Nick said as he took another cigarette from the pack without asking.

We both laughed and, for an instant, I forgot where we were and why we were there. In that instant, Nick was my brother. Sometimes you know your brother by the blood flowing through your veins, and sometimes you know your brother by the blood that has flowed out of them. This was the lesson that could only be learned in combat.

Groping for the water pitcher on the table, I fumbled with the lid and tried to pour a glass. "Fishing, that's the ticket to the *real* life. I'd like to get up and walk out of here and go fishing. Fuck a bunch of bad memories."

"Here's to good memories," said Nick and picked up a glass, clinking it into mine. "I never went fishing in my whole life, but I loved the rodeo."

"Rodeo?"

"Yeah, man. ROW DAY OH. I come from Texas and not just any old place in Texas either. I'm from Brownsville. My old man had me and my brother on horses before we could piss standing up. By the time I was sixteen, I was winning 4-H events all over the state, calf roping, steer wrestling, and even bronc riding."

"Sounds like an easy way to get busted up."

"So's being in a fucking war." Nick pointed to the space where his right leg should have been. He shook his short brown hair vigorously as if freeing it from bugs and his thick lips took a downward turn, curving in toward the dimple in the middle of his square chin. "I guess I won't have to worry about winning any bronc riding contests again." He smacked the empty bedsheet and looked as if he might begin crying. I watched him closely. Nick didn't really cry, but spoke with his head down, ashamed. "Now, I'm just another pathetic gimp with war stories. Where I live, being crippled is almost as bad as being queer."

"Look on the bright side," I said.

"And what's the bright side?"

"You only have to have one pant leg altered when you buy a new suit . . ."

Nick smiled, ". . . Or tie one shoe."

"You don't ever have to run the obstacle course at Camp LaJeune again."

"I won't ever piss on my right foot when I'm drunk."

"You'll always be eligible for a pity fuck in a hippie commune."

An army nurse walked into the white room, dressed in white herself from her white hat to her milky white stockings. She stood about five feet, five inches tall with red hair pulled tightly back in a bun. Her nose crooked slightly right below her green eyes as if it might have been broken in tomboy play a long time ago and, coupled with her thin red lips and the freckles that dotted its bridge, it gave her a unique appearance. She wasn't exactly supermodel beautiful and her breasts sagged a little, but I followed her movements as if she were a goddess.

She was the first American woman I'd seen while fully conscious in almost a year. There had been triage nurses and surgical nurses at Cam Rahn Bay, but I'd been so disoriented that their faces were shadows in the fog. Here was a real, live woman who spoke my language and smiled without betel nut juice running down her chin. Here was a woman I could take to a movie or get married to. Here was a woman who wouldn't give me the black clap or slit my throat while I slept. Yes, she was a goddess all right, a different type of deity with different powers than Le Ly in the village of Gia Le, and I would worship her even if she never won a beauty contest.

"What are you two laughing so hard about?" Nurse Sarah Johnson spoke softly and smiled. She carried a stainless-steel tray full of syringes to the table between the two beds and set it down with a sharp clang. The noise seemed to surprise her and she shuddered involuntarily like a frightened animal in a corner.

"We're just laughing to keep from crying," said Nick.

"I do that all the time myself. How's our new patient?"

"Okay, but I'm confused about what I'm doing in an army hospital. I'm a marine," I said, hoping the question didn't sound too stupid. After all, I'd spent a year in college and wanted to impress this woman with intellectual curiosity and clever conversation. Who knew what might happen if she liked me. There were always the stories from guys who'd been wounded and returned to duty, tales of nurses giving hand jobs, or even head, to help ease the pain of war.

"We get a lot of you guys. We fix you up as good as new and send you back to your families." She spoke the words like nurses were trained to, but the tone in her voice was hollow and made them sound like they were being yelled down a long drainpipe with a sewage ditch at the end. A fly landed on her forearm and she flailed the air, flinging it back into space. Momentarily confused, the fly hovered, and then dove toward a half-eaten Snickers bar on Nick's side of the table. I rolled up a magazine, swatted hard, and then groaned. Nick laughed as the rolled paper thumped loudly, the nurse jumped backward, and the Dewar's Scotch ad on the back of the magazine became the funeral plot for the fly in a coffin of chocolate.

"That's one gook that won't ambush us when the lights go out," said Nick.

"I hate flies."

"Well, you certainly expressed your hatred eloquently Corporal McGarrah." Nurse Johnson picked up a syringe from the steel tray and soaked a cotton ball with alcohol while she was speaking.

"Hey lieutenant, I've got a really bad cramp in my leg."

"I'm sorry, Nick. Let me give you guys these injections and I'll get some lotion and rub it out for you. Where is it?"

"It's right here, ma'am." Nick grabbed his crotch and smiled. "It's my middle leg, which is now my longest one."

The nurse stepped toward Nick holding the syringe like a dagger.

"How about if I give you your penicillin shot in that middle leg? You know better than to talk to an officer like that. What if one of your women marine officers was here instead of me?"

"It's obvious you ain't ever seen a woman marine, ma'am. I'd never allow one of them the opportunity to get anywhere near my pride and joy."

"Hell no, she hasn't," I said. "I volunteered for 'Nam because it was safer in the jungle than around one of their barracks."

"I've ridden less dangerous bulls, smaller too," said Nick.

For a moment, I believed we could have been anywhere other than where we were. We might have been friends hanging out at Greek's Candy Store, flirting and trying to one-up each other while we waited for Mr. Andriokas to hand us vanilla phosphates, except each of us was connected to the other by the thin smells of isopropyl alcohol and Betadine solution and pain instead of sugar and hair spray and Clearasil.

The laughter stopped abruptly, and we stared at different corners of the white room, embarrassed because our brains had misfired, and we had dared to feel almost innocent once again. Nurse Sarah broke the uncomfortable silence.

"I think you're both full of bullshit." She leaned over and swabbed Nick's ass with the cotton and alcohol. He had bared it and raised it to meet the needle. "However, I'll consider the stress of combat on your comments and probably not have you court martialed or castrated today." No one laughed this time, but Sarah attempted a quiet smile while she slid the needle into flesh and pushed the plunger on the syringe as gently as possible.

"Do you have one for me?" I asked.

"Not right now. Nick gets some different medicine than you. You don't need quite as much, although you'll be getting four shots of penicillin every day."

Sarah picked up the tray and turned to leave. She had other shots to give in other white rooms. It was her job to make each wounded soldier on her floor feel like they were special men, even if they weren't. I appreciated the way she tried to display the proper medical knowledge mixed with the right amount of top-less dancer attitude. It was easy to like her because she'd found a way to distribute emotion equally rather than become really, truly attached to any one, or shut off from everyone.

"You know what that means, don't you?" said Nick.

"Not really."

I ran my right hand slowly over the rough gauze wrapped around my left leg and felt the muscle flinch in expectation. My body had always been thick, but sharply defined from summers of hay baling and baseball, plus autumns of football, and I was famil-iar with it from years of adolescent narcissism. I continued along the leg's contour surveying the damage by touch. Everything was covered in cotton and wrapped with gauze. Right in the middle, a plastic shunt connected the wound that was beneath the gauze to a plastic tube running into a plastic bag filling with blood mixed with a yellow viscous liquid. An IV bottle hung on a stainless steel rack that had been rolled between the head of the bed and the night table. It attached itself to me by means of another long plas-tic tube and a needle running into my vein on the back of my hand. A saline solution dripped into my arm. There was no flesh to touch on my left leg at all, but underneath the bandages, the constant tingle of a thousand hot needles.

"Not really he says. Well, let me educate you, Jimmy boy. The gooks piss all over their RPGs and land mines, so when you get a load of shrapnel like you did, your blood gets full of gook piss and you die of blood poisoning without antibiotics. So you get plenty of penicillin. Ain't that right, Lieutenant?"

"I wouldn't call that the textbook answer Nick, but it's pretty accurate."

Sarah's eyebrows came together like red rogue caterpillars in heat. She laughed again.

"I just want to make sure I'm getting everything I need. I don't trust the Marine Corps anymore," I said. "They obviously don't have my best interest at heart."

"Remember, I'm an *army* nurse and this is an army hospital."

Nick grunted. "Now there's a big comfort."

The nurse left the room before I could respond, speaking over her shoulder as she turned down the hall, "I'll be back soon with the pain medicine."

*   *   *

It was impossible to tell daylight from dark in the white room. Most people defined blindness as blackness, an absence of colors, forms, and shapes. But what if blindness was really white, all the colors of the spectrum combining to make any single color indistinguishable? Maybe that's why I'd always misunderstood good and evil. Evil wore black. Wickedness manifested itself in harsh colors of all kinds, or so I believed in the much simpler time of childhood. Hopalong Cassidy and the Lone Ranger rode white horses, Topper and Silver. In every cowboy movie I saw that starred either John Wayne or Gene Autry, the good guys were easily recognizable because they wore white hats. Even the Cisco Kid's horse was a pinto, which meant it had white spots. It could only be partially white because Cisco wasn't one hundred percent pure American.

The villains dressed in black hats and did vile things to women and horses, but the white-hatted heroes always made them pay. Even when President John F. Kennedy spoke of the communists, they were the red menace and a black blight on freedom. Che Guevera sported a black beret in news photos. Lee Harvey Oswald owned several black T-shirts and was photographed for *Life* magazine wearing one. Even this war had started with the Domino Theory and dominoes were black. All the people I'd ever trusted, especially my father, said these people and things were the dark forces, blind to the American way of life, the right way of life, freedom and goodness, and though Dad didn't want me to go to this war, I could sense the pride in the tone of his letters that he had a son fighting communism. Morality was absolutely white for me before I came to the jungle. Duty remained clear in terms of all versus nothing, good versus evil. The world was without shades or nuances of color. There were no rainbows for an American. The Vietcong wore black pajamas.

Had I been able to keep my mental focus on this distinction, I might still have defined good and evil simply and without reservation for all time. The doubts that caused as much pain as the wounds would never have been born. But months of watching the people in the black pajamas bleed and die, scream and cry the same way the good guys did blurred my perception. I was guilty of the mistake no soldier can afford to make. I began to see my enemy as humans who had families and frailties, who got hungry and drunk, who believed in what they did. Then there was the boy, the barber's son, and there was the strange way Rick Santos died. They changed the way I would see and define colors and the world forever. Life had stirred the palette and shaded the tones. Now, even in this white room, hurting and not knowing if it was day or night or if my pain was good or bad, my eyes were veiled with gray.

Pressure built in the back of my head as if someone had shoved an iron pipe through the base of my skull. Small spots the color of smoked salmon floated in front of my eyes. Some questions should never be asked, and some questions should never have to be answered.

In the background, clipped and harsh syllables of Japanese filtered from the suspended television set. *Bonanza* had been replaced by something that seemed like a sports show. Ignoring Nick, I tried to focus on the small screen. A stadium full of people surrounded a cage that rose from the center of a stage. The audience sat on platformed tiers rather than the hardback folding seats found in an American auditorium and they were all dressed in robes—kimonos, I'd heard them called in Okinawa. The announcer strutted back and forth, an oriental Mick Jagger, clapping his hands and firing the audience into an evangelical type of fervor.

Two other men wheeled a smaller cage to the open door of the larger one and raised the door on it. A tiger leapt out and immediately began to pace the length of the bigger cage, first straight across, then in diagonals and finally circling the inside perimeter. It measured its prison and roared. The crowd roared with it. A hush settled over the entire arena. A tiny man who closely resembled a piece of overcooked gristle stepped onto the stage and bowed to the announcer. He turned and bowed to the audience, and then to the tiger, his long, thin white hair falling forward across his eyes. The man wore the traditional Okinawa style of the *keiko gi*, a plain white cotton shirt and pants very similar to the hospital pajamas I had on. The only color other than the man's copper face was a bright red sash around his lean waist.

He stepped into the cage and instantly transformed from a wizened old man into a graceful dancer, moving around the tiger in ever-tightening circles. The tiger followed the man's movements warily, but with the disdain that comes from power. Soon, as if hypnotized by the man's movements, the tiger began to move with him. They were connected by a rhythm that preceded humanity and transcended thought. I understood what was happening even though the language of the announcer, who now whispered into his microphone, was unintelligible. I understood it because I had waltzed this same waltz in the jungle. The music played internally and only the combatants could hear it. It was beauty, truth, love, and the incredible natural buildup of electricity that would cause one of these dancers to explode first. This waltz was part of a natural symphony, the prelude to violent death.

Without warning, without twitch of tail or ear or whisker, the tiger leapt. The little Japanese man dropped to one knee and, when the thousand pounds of muscle was directly over him, his right arm shot upward so fast that the television camera almost couldn't follow it. The tiger sailed past the man and fell motionless to the floor. The man stood and held a football-sized object in his hand. As the camera zoomed in, I felt my stomach tighten as if driving fast over a sharp hill. The tiger's heart, quivering slightly, filled the screen. At first, I thought it might be some kind of a trick, some magical surrealism intended to satisfy the audience's obvious bloodlust. It couldn't be real. They weren't allowed to show things like that on screen. Hell, if it was illegal to fight dogs and cocks, then it had to be illegal to butcher a beautiful, graceful animal in this manner.

Then I remembered that this wasn't American television and that different cultures had different values. It was real, just as real as the bullfight I would witness the first time I made a road trip to Mexico four summers later after being discharged from the marines. The sickness in my stomach subsided and I began to wonder how people in this part of the world felt about me traveling ten thousand miles to burn a child, blow up their paddies, torch their hooches, screw their young women, and sacrifice my own men to Lyndon B. Johnson and Tricky Dick Nixon, the American gods of such activity. I still felt sorry for the tiger but, in the grand scheme of things, some ethics professor at some junior college would be hard pressed to defend one thing against the other.

"What's so funny? You think it's *funny* that I'm a one-legged gimp?"

"I wasn't laughing at you, Nick. I was laughing at the television."

"Don't laugh at me or I'll kick your ass."

I sat up in bed and started to stand. An urge rose in me, the one that must have overtaken the little Japanese man in the tiger's cage. It was more than survival. It was the desire to best an opponent. It was the desire to prove myself still a man. I would have hit Nick in the face, but pain held me back.

"Easy, pardner. Lay back down and take a deep breath before you bleed all over me. Two gimps fighting is an ugly sight," said Nick.

"Look, I just don't want to talk about the war or think about it. I made mistakes and I did the best I could to get home alive and sane, like you. You must have done some things that you don't like thinking about, made some mistakes."

"The only mistake I made was following the orders of a fucked-up corporal. It don't take a genius to order a squad around a minefield instead of *through* it. Is that the kind of mistakes that got made in your case?"

Sweat rolled off my forehead. I clenched the bedsheets and tried to push up again. I felt dizzy, and worse, knew Nick noticed my weakness. The private wouldn't leave me alone. Once you find the enemy's weakness, you must move in for the kill. We were both trained this way. It was what made marines so good at war and so guilty after, the focus on the kill, on making it instantly and without thought.

"I'm just saying, don't laugh at me, motherfucker. I'm as good a man as you'll ever be." Nick turned toward me.

Grabbing the only thing I could reach, I flung the magazine I had used to swat the fly at Nick's head.

"Fuck you," said Nick, as he ducked and the magazine knocked over the plastic water pitcher on the table. Water splattered us both and the pitcher rolled across the buffed tile floor.

"Fuck *you*, you one-legged cocksucker."

Nick's eyes drifted away. The fire had gone from them and, for an instant, he seemed to have that faraway stare of the dying that I had become so familiar with these past few months. Suddenly, he began to scream at the ceiling, no longer concerned that another person was in the room. The argument was over, and not because I had convinced Nick I wasn't ridiculing him. I knew it, but felt thankful just the same.

"Oh shit. Fuck. Piss. Suck my dick, bitch. Where's my shot?"

"What the hell's wrong with you? You just got a shot."

"You'll see. Oh yeah, you'll see once you been here a while."

"See what?"

"Time. You learn to tell time by the shots."

"You are one fucked-up jarhead. You can't tell time with penicillin."

"Not those shots, asshole. The dope, man, morphine. *Hurry up bitch.*" Nick's face turned colorless like bleached flour. He flicked the call button over and over as fast as his thumb could move. His pale blue hospital gown darkened with sweat. "Gimme my shot."

At first, it seemed that Nick's groans echoed off the walls and down the long corridor of the ward outside the white room. Moaning floated on the air as if a storm were rising in an exotic harbor somewhere and the wind plucked the cables of a dozen moored boats while the boats strained to break free. When Nurse Johnson opened the door and ran in the room, I realized that the noise was not an echo but rather a chorus of bedridden wounded in the ward outside our room.

"Quiet down, Nick. You're not the only one on this floor of the hospital who's in pain, and all this yelling just gets everybody upset," she said as she extracted a syringe and needle from the front waist pocket of her white uniform.

"You're late. You're always late. My leg is killing me and by God my leg tells time better than the goddamn cheap Timex on your wrist."

"Watch your mouth. I told you to calm down. If you don't be quiet, I'm leaving. I'll call the doctor and you can wait for him to get here to give you your shot."

Nick's agitation ceased immediately. He had been a child who couldn't hold his water a few seconds before and now, he was a child who had wet the bed and lay frozen in shame. His voice sang in the tinny falsetto of regret.

"You wouldn't do that, would you?"

A slight smirk tightened the nurse's lips. It was a sneer of satisfaction that comes from the exercise of absolute power, and when I noticed it, my lust and love and adoration for her mixed with cold fear. It was almost a religious experience.

"That's better," she said. "Besides, your leg doesn't really hurt. It can't. You're just feeling ghost pain." The moans outside had settled into a collective hum, a rhythmic background to the litany of well-practiced words the nurse spoke. "You stepped on a land mine three weeks ago, remember? I keep telling you this same thing every day. Your mind wants the shot, the rest of your body wants the shot, but not your leg. Anyone who goes through this kind of trauma is eligible for ghost pain. The pain is real, but the cause of it no longer exists. And if the doctor doesn't quit prescribing these morphine shots for you soon, whatever VA hospital you end up in is going to have a drug addict to deal with. You know what I'm telling you is true."

The concern, the self-sacrifice, the expression of a woman who lives to be needed, returned to Nurse Johnson's face. The cruelty that flushed her cheeks only seconds before had dissipated in the ambiguous fog between language and action as she injected the opiate into Nick's arm. She sat the syringe on the night table and fluffed his pillows as he sighed and crooned to her in the soft voice of a man to whom she had given all she had to give.

"Say what you will. It knows." Nick's arm floated slowly above his body like an unmoored skiff in the ocean and he pointed to the space below his thigh. "It knows what time it is."

Nurse Johnson took another syringe from her pocket and prepared to inject me.

"If I'm going to be like that in another week, then get that shit away from me. I'm Irish. Bring me some whiskey for my pain."

"It's standard procedure to treat you guys with antibiotics and morphine."

"Why? So you can keep us quiet?"

"We want you to be able to fight off infection and to stay comfortable too. Besides," she shook her head as if she didn't want to believe her own words, "the docs don't mind extending the length of days for the morphine. They believe you guys have earned it."

"I don't want to be a damn junkie."

"The choice is pretty much yours, I guess. You tell me you don't want anymore of this and I make a note on your chart. The doctor comes around tomorrow and asks you how you feel and you say the pain is manageable. It's that simple. But, tonight I have orders and you're going to get the shot."

"How do you make a choice not to get in trouble if you're already in trouble?"

"That's one of the great mysteries in life. I will tell you this—at some point, the military will stop the morphine, either before you get sent back to your unit, or before you get discharged from the service. If you don't want another big problem to deal with in the near future, you might start thinking about that now. Nick doesn't give a damn, do you, Nick?"

The needle stung and the morphine burned its way through my upper right arm. I began losing control very quickly and hated that feeling. If you can't control a situation, you can't control the outcome of it. That was the very reason I'd used both drugs and alcohol in moderation while fighting the war. I suffered from the illusion that my destiny was dictated by my own actions. Frightened, I curled into a fetal position and barely heard Nick's slurred answer.

"I don't want to think about the two-legged future I don't have. I'm sticking with Gracie Slick's philosophy—'it don't mean shit to a tree.'"

"Lights out in thirty minutes. If you guys are going to write any letters, you better get started. Leave them on the table and I'll pick them up right before my shift ends."

Nick waved feebly.

"Thanks for the cocktail, Nurse Sweetie."

* * *

Demons and witches have no backs. They have faces on both sides. I tried to remember if I'd ever seen the back of Sarah Johnson's head. She always walked into the room and kind of sidled out of it crablike. She could have been a witch because I felt bewitched as the morphine began to massage my brain. Can something, anything, be complete in your mind if you can only see the front side? Maybe. The last moon I saw hung over the jungle in Thua Thien province. That moon was full, but *full* was inadequate to describe its ripeness. On this particular night, the moon had become complete. It filled with the sense of being big and round, it filled with color, first orange and then white-grape yellow. It filled with expectation, promise, and the reflected light of the sun. It filled with artificial life. But what had drawn me to the moon that particular night was its fullness beyond my means to express. This moon lifted me into a realm where untouchable things lived, shadows with substance, an energy unseen and untasted but more complete than any concept of any god I'd ever read about. It pulled on me as if I was connected to all the tides in all the oceans.

The feeling that crept over me now was complete like that moon, even though I only saw the moon's face. I could touch everything around and in me, even pain. I could get inside the drug, examine it, *be* it and at the same time distance myself from it. It connected me to a place where pain existed as useless afterthought. I began to evolve from all life into all life, and finally, into something more than life. It was the first time since being wounded that I'd consciously let anyone give me morphine, and it was the light from that moon over Thua Thien captured in a syringe. I floated in its warm, heavy syrup of numbness and as Sarah Johnson's face, the one that made her a witch capable of holding the moon in her hands, the one that must have existed on both sides of her head, drifted disembodied out of the white room, my own head nodded and my eyes began to uncontrollably close.

*   *   *

"Hey. Hey. You gonna write any letters, man?"

The white room reappeared as blackness. Small patches of yellow light filtered in under the closed door at different angles as someone walked into an office or a bathroom in the hallway outside.

"Hey. Hey, wake up. Let's write a letter," said Nick again.

"What the fuck. What time is it?"

A phosphorescent flying saucer landed on my chest. I picked it up and read the glowing dial from Nick's watch. 2:30 a.m.

"Jesus," I said. "We were supposed to write letters four hours ago before the lights went out."

"Keep your voice down, asshole. I got a flashlight."

There was a quick click and a white beam hit me in the face. "Shit." Nick turned the flashlight on its end and set it on the table. The beam spread out across the ceiling in a circle the size of a basketball.

"That's enough light. I been trying to write a letter for two weeks," said Nick.

"Girlfriend?" I asked, still groggy from the morphine injection.

"Fuck no. How's a gimp like me gonna find a new girlfriend? Mine sent me a 'Dear John' letter two days after I shipped out for 'Nam. I'll be paying for my pussy from now on. That's one of the fortunes of war, man. I gotta tell my dad that my leg's gone and that's really gonna piss him off. You can't hop around a ranch and get the work done."

"Didn't the Marine Corps inform him when you were hit?"

"The Corps doesn't tell your loved ones you've got parts missing. It's bad for the image."

"This whole fucking war is about image."

The sound of flint scraping filled the silence and the flame from the Zippo illuminated Nick's face. He nodded and inhaled deeply as another of my Winstons glowed. "Now you got it. The Marine Corps is just like the Boy Scouts, except the scouts have adult leaders. Nobody thinks in the Corps. So, here I am left to break the news to my family that I'm gonna be a cripple for the rest of my life. How the hell do you explain that, especially to a man who gets up before dawn every fucking morning and works till dark? I don't ever remember him even being sick. Hell, he complains all the time about welfare loafers who invent excuses not to work and live off his tax money. Wait till he finds out that I'm getting a big disability check every month. He'll bitch that it's coming right out of his pocket."

"Tell him the truth. For Christ's sake, he's your father."

"The truth doesn't always fix things," said Nick.

"Try it and see. You write your dad and I'll write a letter that I don't want to write."

"A sweet thing from Princeton, Indiana?" asked Nick as he snubbed the cigarette out.

"I only wish. No, this one guy in my squad was a special friend. He was my brother; you know how it is in combat. You just hit it off with one guy. He's got your back and you got his. Evidently, I didn't have his too well, did I? Anyway, he was our corpsman. I promised him if anything happened I'd let his parents know the truth about how he bought it. He was six days from the world, man. Six fucking days."

"Shit, that's some serious bad luck. Why write? They know by now he was wasted and they sure as hell don't know you made that promise. Why put yourself through more fucking grief?"

"Because I know I made the promise. When you're responsible for keeping someone alive and you let him down, the memory sticks to your brain like one of those big Mekong river leeches. It sucks the life out of you and won't let go."

"Then, you better write the letter, man."

"Yeah. I'd better write the fucking letter."

* * *

Dear Dad,

Remember when we spoke on the phone when I first got to Japan . . .

Dear Mr. and Mrs. Santos,

You don't know me, but Rick may have mentioned me in his letters . . .

. . . Dad, I told you I was doing okay. I am doing okay because I'm alive. But, okay is all I'm doing. Something bad happened when I got wounded and I don't know exactly how to explain it. Remember the time that two-year-old colt of mine got horny and tried to mount the John Deere? He broke his leg and was useless . . .

. . . I was Rick's friend for the short time we knew each other in Vietnam. We were close friends . . .

. . .and when the vet came out to put him to sleep, I cried for two days and you got mad because you said that men shouldn't cry when bad things happen. Well, I'm not crying now, but I feel like it. It turns out that I'm going to be kind of useless around the ranch just like that colt . . .

. . . I even made sure that Montengard bracelet he bought in Da Nang was with his stuff. He was real proud of that bracelet and said it would look beautiful on his mom's wrist. I hope you got it all right. He loved you a lot and made me promise to write this letter if something happened to him . . .

. . . Dad, the Marine Corps probably told you I was wounded in my leg. That's true. But it was worse than that. My leg is gone and I don't know what to do about it. I feel like I let you down . . .

. . . I feel like I really let him down. He was packing his bags to come home and a sniper snuck into range . . .

. . .I was just trying to be a good marine, Dad, like we talked about when I enlisted. I tried to do a good job. We were chasing two gook zappers who ran across a rice paddy into the jungle and I was the point man. I didn't want to cross the paddy. I had a funny feeling about it, but my squad leader said we had to. I had to go first and the paddy was mined . . .

. . . I heard a shot and when I got to our bunker, Rick had been hit. We were all afraid because we didn't know for sure where the shot came from at first. But we found the sniper and . . .

. . .You warned me not to volunteer for anything, Dad, but what choice did I have? I was told that my action saved the rest of the squad, but the only action I remember is an explosion, a scream, flying through the air, and landing in the mud. I remember not crying, though. I didn't cry. I hope you won't hate me because this happened . . .

. . . I feel responsible because we found him too late. If it helps, Rick saved a lot of people. He was a fine medic and a good, kind man. It's been very hard to sleep knowing Rick's dead and I'm not. I'm sure he died loving you and you can be proud of the way he died.

. . . Dad, it's very hard to sleep since this happened. They give me medicine and it helps some. I'll be coming home soon.

Your son, Nick
Your friend, Lance Corporal James E. McGarrah

* * *

I folded the letter as Nick began to snore again. Looking over in the dim glow of the flashlight, I set the letter on the table and noticed the pen still wrapped in Nick's fingers and the pad of paper resting on his chest. I wanted to sleep like him and flicked the flashlight switch. There was something about the day that Rick died that drained the very essence of being from my soul. The light tumbled into the cylinder and the room went black again. I played the scene over and over in my head, the sound of the shot, the angle of entry, the calm on Rick's face, the rifle between his knees. Maybe the light wasn't really *off*, just imprisoned by the aluminum tube. That's why the batteries went dead even if no one used the flashlight. They used all their energy keeping the light in.

The rhythm of Nick's relaxed snoring should have been enough to rock me to sleep, but every time I closed my eyes another sound drowned the snoring out. At first, I didn't recognize it or where it came from. It seemed to originate inside my head and, at the same time, be outside in the room. Soon, the sound broke apart into many sounds and the many sounds molded themselves into a pattern, and then the pattern became words.

"Nick. Nick, what did you say?"

The snoring continued evenly in the bed next to mine. At first, curiosity stirred, but all that separated curiosity from fear was a thin wall of perception that could easily be penetrated by reality. What about the time I had been on Operation Lancaster out in the bush for three weeks? The squad dug in one night a few clicks outside our base camp at the Rockpile, and the minute my ass hit the bottom of his foxhole, I fell asleep. A slight tingling across both legs woke me. The movement tickled more than anything and I started to giggle. Reaching into the shirt pocket of my sweaty jungle fatigues, I pulled out the old Zippo. When the soft yellow light filled the bottom of the hole, my curiosity sent a surge of electricity up the spine, and electric curiosity in the jungle is just another way to describe terror. A Russell's viper, about three feet long, slithered across my boot tops. Fortunately, light seemed to frighten the snake almost as much as its poison frightened me and it shot out the top of the foxhole, sliding into the elephant grass with the sound of dry leaves rustling across asphalt. I trembled for what seemed a long time, and then lit and relit the Zippo all night until the lighter fluid ran out. I felt that similar need for light now, in my hospital bed.

I fumbled around on the nightstand and finally hit the switch on the cold, metal tube. Released, the beam of light shot over Nick's sleeping face and ricocheted off the wall. I grabbed the flashlight and flung the beam around the room in wide, desperate arcs. There was no one else, and the words disappeared. Still, they had come from someone somewhere. The door remained closed. The chair was empty. Nurse Johnson had turned off the television several hours before. I was wide awake now and the slight tremble had returned to my arms, so even when I tried to hold the light steady, it danced slightly against the white walls. Setting the flashlight back on the table to steady the beam, I decided that it would be a bad idea to allow darkness the chance to bring the voice back. I hit the call button for Nurse Johnson, thinking I might use the bedpan. I could have held it until she made her rounds, but it seemed important to speak with a real person, even if it was only to ask for a cold, stainless steel can to piss into. I suddenly felt like a small boat on a swelling sea and when Sarah opened the door, the light washed in from the hallway, almost capsizing me.

"What are you doing awake?" she asked.

"I have to use the bathroom."

She handed me the object from a table against the wall on the right side of the room. "Do you need any help?"

The questioned embarrassed me. I was used to women handling my dick, especially for money, but not for this purpose. The idea that I couldn't take care of myself humiliated me, made me feel less than what I'd always been taught a man should be.

"Why would I need help to take a piss, for God's sake?"

Nurse Johnson flinched and stepped back slightly in the shadowed light. She didn't seem afraid as much as she seemed wary, like a boxer who can take a punch because he knows how to prepare for one.

"Something on your mind?" she asked, quietly.

"No. I'm fine. That dumb ass snores too loud for me to sleep. That's all."

"Would you like me to put a pillow over his head and press down?"

The tension broke. I felt a smile inching across my face. Maybe she felt it too, even in the dark.

"I don't suppose you could stay for a while."

"Jim, I'm in the middle of rounds right now. I've got twenty-seven other guys to check on. I could come back in a little while, if you want."

"That's alright. I'm going to try to go back to sleep."

Nurse Johnson closed the door on her way out, and as soon as she did, I turned the flashlight back off. Setting the bedpan unused on the floor, I listened. The voice had come back. It was real and present. It had a texture I couldn't ignore any longer, so rather than scream into the blank night, I answered it.

"What do you want?"

"Are you going to lay there and try to have a conversation with a dead man? Jesus, what an idiot."

The voice belonged to Rick. I'd have known that voice anywhere, the slight nasal twang, the upward lilt at the end of each sentence and the sarcastic bite of someone who knew you better than you knew yourself. I searched the shadows for a body to attach the voice to. The shadows rustled along the walls. Something was hidden in each one, but whatever was in them was out of reach, and it wasn't a friend. Maybe I had gone over the edge. It happened to men in combat all the time. The eyes were never meant to see the things seen or the conscience made to condone the things done. Okay. I was crazy. No, that wouldn't work. I couldn't be crazy and think I was crazy at the same time. Maybe the voice came from somewhere inside me. No. That wouldn't work either. My father always told me that if you asked yourself a question and then answered, you *were* crazy.

"Are you an angel?"

"Are you nuts? Now, tell me why you didn't let my parents know what really happened to me."

"Knowing more than what I told them wouldn't help them deal with death. People in the world don't know how to live with death."

"Why? It's a simple question."

"Simple questions don't always have simple answers."

"Yes, they do. It's just that the answers are sometimes unpleasant."

"A sniper killed you."

"If you were sure of that, I wouldn't be here."

"*I am sure.*"

"No. There's some small part of your mind holding onto the idea something else happened. Maybe, just maybe, if you'd paid more attention to the things I said and did you could have stopped me."

"Stopped you from what?"

"You know what."

"No. I don't."

"Yes, you do. By the way, hold your voice down. You might wake up your junkie buddy over there."

"There was no way you could have done that. The NVA sniper came up into the temple."

"And shot me in the face from behind? No. You covered the truth. I was trying to make an important statement about what war does to men and you took the opportunity away from me."

"I made the right call. You would have done the same thing in my place."

My mind focused on the scene. A mist of smoke lingered in the silence. Then I was with Rick, sitting next to him on the edge of the trench. There were tears in his eyes. He placed the rifle stock on the ground between his feet and aimed the flash suppressor toward his chin. Rick squeezed the trigger carefully, as if the trigger might bruise his finger, and closed his eyes.

"You may never admit what I did, but you'll know, and what'll keep eating you alive is the why. You just can't quite get it."

Nick began to toss and turn in his bed. He moaned and sat up.

"Halt motherfucker. Who goes there? What's the password?" said Nick.

"Hey, be quiet. You'll wake up the goddamn ward yelling like that."

"Get away from me. You can't have it."

I looked at Nick in disbelief. "Can't have what?"

"My leg, you prick. It's mine. Give it back."

"I don't have your leg. You left it in a rice paddy, you idiot."

Nick rubbed his eyes, opened them, and seemed to notice my presence, but it was impossible to tell if he recognized who I was.

"Huh. Where am I?"

"In la-la land. Now go back to sleep before Nurse Johnson comes in and gags you. You were just dreaming."

"I heard someone talking."

"Me. I was talking to you."

"No, I heard something else."

"Yeah, two marbles rolling together between your ears. Go back to sleep."

"I swear I heard another voice. I want my leg back."

Nick rolled away toward the opposite wall and was soon snoring again. I lit a cigarette and waited. At first, all I heard was the smoke as it hissed from my lungs and out of my mouth. Then Rick came back.

"What a basket case. Keep taking your morphine, McGarrah. That's you pretty soon."

"I'll never be like that."

"I felt invincible once. We fool ourselves all the time. It's our nature."

"Not me."

"Right. Now, you were about to tell me why you lied to my mom and dad."

"How could I tell them this is what you planned?"

"Quit bullshitting me. I didn't plan to do what I did. I was just too tired to go on, and it seemed like the right thing to do in the moment."

An inexplicable phenomenon began to take place in the dim glow of the flashlight. At first, I thought I might be hallucinating because a backlit shadow, almost like a jack-o-lantern, appeared in the chair next to the bed. I dismissed that thought. It was too frightening. It would have meant that control of the situation had been lost. As long as I accepted the voice and now the face, as real, however unnatural, that meant that my mind was intact and, as long as I kept acting as if everything was quite normal it would, in fact, be normal. Somebody could somehow explain whatever strange things were happening to me at a later time, but I would understand those explanations better if I didn't freak out at the present time and end up in a psycho ward. There were all kinds of stories about people who had seen flying saucers and ghosts—too many to be discounted—and how many times had I been set up in a late-night ambush with all kinds of things moving through the dark air that had no substance but still existed—elephants, bugs, VC, tigers, snakes. Our radioman, Ron Johnson, had even seen a

Spanish dancer and, when four other guys heard castanets clacking, nobody could argue the point.

So I continued the conversation with my dead friend named Rick as if the man were really there and slowly he appeared in the chair beside me. Bedsheets rustled. Nick sat straight up and whispered hoarsely, "*Incoming. Incoming. Fire in the hole.*"

"Jesus. Stuff a sock in it, will ya?" said Rick.

"He can't hear you."

"That's my problem—nobody can except you. The only thing left of me is in your morphine soaked mind."

"I couldn't tell your parents or anyone else. I wanted them to get your insurance money. At least they'd have something and the whole thing wouldn't seem so god-awful useless."

"That's the point, Jimbo. It *is* all useless. The whole fucking thing is useless."

"I heard you. I heard you talking to someone, motherfucker," said Nick, still sitting upright in his bed. He was sweating again, but he was really awake this time. Nick picked up the flashlight and flung the beam viciously around the room. "Who's there?" There was metal and wood and plastic and white emptiness.

"See? Nothing. I told you you were dreaming. Now for Christ's sake go back to sleep and leave me alone. I feel like shit and you're making me feel worse by talking."

"I could use another shot myself."

"Of morphine?"

"No, jerk off, monkey urine. Of course, morphine."

I trembled and was sweating like Nick. The pain ran, galloped, along my left side again, and my head throbbed. Maybe I'd dreamt the whole sequence with Rick, maybe it didn't happen. On the other hand, what did Nick keep hearing? That dumb ass heard a voice too. Hell, morphine didn't sound like a bad idea. I pressed the call button for Nurse Johnson and waited in silence with my one-legged roommate, wondering if I believed that my friend had actually killed himself and, at the same time, knowing that he did. Thirty years has passed since that night in the Camp Drake Army Hospital, and I still fight that infectious ambivalence.

Chapter 15

A TEMPORARY SORT OF PEACE

The car slipped deep within one of those gunmetal-blue Mexican nights. The insane rumble of a semi, aglow with Christmas tree lights and the skeletal grin of the driver, rattled the windows as it roared past. We were on Highway 57 somewhere between Saltillo and Matehuela. Above us, the stars clustered like quartz in a candlelit cave. Around us, the Madonna danced naked on the truck's passing dashboard. A young man named Jack sat stoically behind the wheel of the 1964 Oldsmobile Cutlass. I owned the car and leaned forward in the front seat, waiting for Jack to notice a single steer standing on the road. A plump man called Basil stretched out across the back seat asleep.

"Don't you see a cow with horns on the road in front of us?"

"Is it real?" Jack answered.

"Is it real? What the hell kind of a question are you asking me, 'Is it real?'"

"It's hard to tell when things are really out there. I'm taking my stay-awake pills and they sure do keep me awake. But sometimes, I see things moving around and when I get to them they're not there. It's confusing, like waiting for God to give you a sign and then the cops break in the door to your apartment and you have to flush your stash. You know what I mean?"

Jack believed No-Doz and mescaline were synonyms. Considering the number of tabs he dropped when we crossed the border several hours ago, it was a miracle he didn't mistake the steer for a drunken alien. I had known him only slightly before we left upstate New York the day before yesterday, but Basil, a close and trusted associate, insisted that Jack had an uncanny aptitude for driving long distances. What my Greek friend didn't mention was that this aptitude wasn't genetic in origin. I finally realized it was chemical. Jack's body drove for hours without his mind knowing it.

"It's not moving. It's not moving. Is it moving?" I shouted.

Jack never acknowledged my voice, but the tone of it seemed to drag the car down to a slow crawl. Basil awoke in time to watch a thousand-pound steer roll over the windshield, the roof, and down the back glass. It landed on all fours. Basil began to scream as the huge beast shook its head and gave the halted car a dazed stare.

"Jesus Christ! Was that some kind of animal?"

"Jim said it was a cow with horns, or a horny cow, I can't remember," said Jack, who had yet to blink. "Probably jumped a fence someplace. It doesn't look hurt to me. I was only going ten miles an hour when I hit it. Probably just got a real good rush."

"Let me explain it one more time to both you assholes. There are no fences to jump in Mexico. Animals graze wherever they find grass. They're the pedestrians of the range. Pedestrians have the right of way. Don't you idiots fuck up my vacation." Basil shook his head and looked dazed, like the cow.

Highway 57 writhed toward Mexico City, shedding the Olds like a used snakeskin. Darkness was a spent squeezebox, collapsing in silence around the three of us. By dawn, the car overheated. We were climbing. The air was thin. The car was too damaged to function properly, even at low speed. The steer had gored the radiator, given it a coronada, a great belly wound as if it were Manolete in the bullring. I knew that because I had just finished reading *Death in the Afternoon*. I loved Hemingway, not so much for his words as for his life and his death.

The engine struggled, but it was a losing fight. We stopped at every service station on the road during the hundred-mile ascent into the city. Small brown men with black moustaches swarmed over the car carrying buckets of foul water, which they dumped on the radiator. The hot metal hissed. The engine sputtered and died. The men grabbed the radiator cap like they were reaching in a rattlesnake hole and twisted. Steam squeezed around the edges of the cap. In an instant, the pressure was gone. They refilled the tank, took their ten-peso tip and smiled knowingly while the three gringos drove away.

"That's not a bad gig, you know," said Jack.

"What's not?"

"Oh hell. Don't get this fool started, Jim. He'll spend the next three hundred miles explaining the Zen implications of carrying water buckets, and he has no idea what Zen is."

Basil had warned me before we left New York about Jack's pre-occupation with the reality of nothingness. And it was true—the pale man could talk for hours, and like a reptile, his vacant eyes never blinked. On the other hand, Basil analyzed, philosophized, and reconstructed the patterns of reality constantly, as if by discussing it thoroughly, life could be lived. I wanted to violently shake both of them simply because neither one had a clue. There were times when the jungle in Vietnam had been so quiet that I heard myself sweating, and the air so thick it felt like wet paste on my face. Those were the times when I saw death come by sniper, by rocket, or bayonet. Those were the times I had to ask the question, "Why him and not me?" I understood that the answer was beyond my grasp, but the question never let me go, anymore than that single gunshot four years in the past or the flat, blank stare of Rick Santos ever let me sleep a full night through. At least Rick was a memory now and not with me in person like he was in the early days at Camp Drake Hospital when I swore my mind had slipped a cog.

Now, I was just tired and afraid that I might one day go insane again if I couldn't learn to stop remembering. My two companions had missed the Vietnam War by the luck of the draw. I wasn't bitter about that. But their concepts of what life was all about, though radically different to them, were the same to me—silly.

The sun rose in Mexico City, an ugly, dusty, pink ball filtered through several layers of smog. Basil and Jack slept soundly while the mountain wind wheezed as it pushed salmon-colored air over Chapultepec Park. Beneath a stone monument, the black earth was digesting bones of children. The Olds inched by the main gate, pinched between a Fiat and a dented Volvo. I felt trapped and sick to my stomach, as if I had just driven over Fishers Hill in Princeton, Indiana, and the road dropped away from the wheels too quickly.

When I went through boot camp at Parris Island in 1967, the battle of Chapultepec was required reading. From the perspective of the Marine Corps, as young men were trained for the war in Vietnam, this historic place was a monument to the bravery and honor of a few good men. Semper Fidelis. From a Mexican perspective, a few good men had slaughtered hundreds of peons, young and old alike, without restraint or remorse. I hated myself for thinking about this crap. The only reasonable way to look at this stuff was through the bottom of an empty tequila bottle.

"Jim. Jim McGarrah. Earth to asshole!" Basil awoke, screaming again.

"What?"

"I can always tell when you're thinking about Vietnam. You get this look on your face like you just slept with your mother."

"I did sleep with yours before we left New York. She's still a sloppy lay."

"To hell with you."

"Hell you."

"I'm serious, man. It's over for you. You came home on a stretcher but you were still breathing. It's four years over for you. You came up to New York a speed freak burned out on life who needed a place to hide. It's good that you kicked the speed, but you're still hiding. You need to talk to someone."

"Basil, my friend, if I talk to a shrink, he's going to claim that feeling this way is normal and I just need to hug my father. If I talk to a VA counselor, he's going to claim I'm faking a problem so I can get on disability and not have to work for a living."

"You don't work anyway, except for those horses you green break for Miller Riding Stable when you feel the need to punish yourself."

"I can't focus on steady work, and I like being on the back of a thousand-pound animal that wants to get me off. It's a challenge to stay on. Everything else you call work bores me."

Basil was ten years older than me. His parents had been immigrants and he had grown up believing in the American Dream that any poor boy could become a capitalist in the best sense of the word, an entrepreneur and philanthropist, a liberal thinker and conservative economist, a romantic pragmatist. He was compassionate, thoughtful, a fat slob who smoked too much, and full of brilliant ideas that often destroyed his bank account when he put them into action. He was my good friend and I loved him. I still love him, although he died of heart failure before reaching the age of fifty.

"Where are we?" Jack asked.

We had stopped at a small, open bar on the southwest side of Mexico City. It was 10:00 a.m. and very hot. Several dusty men sat beneath a tin awning, and overhead a fan with a bad bearing hummed loudly. It made the only noise in the place. I knew what

I wanted, and what I wanted, I needed. Behind a piece of rough-hewn wood, a bartender waited.

"Por yo, uno cerveza and uno Cuervo por fa-vore."

"You want a beer and a shot of tequila?"

"You speak English?"

"A lot better than you speak Spanish, amigo. I played soccer for a year at Cal State."

"What are you doing here?"

"My parents own the place and I get free drinks."

Jack and Basil ordered Pacifico beer. I drank Bohemia. We waited in silence for the bottles to empty so we could start again.

* * *

From the bar, the road ran south toward the coast. Jack and Basil sipped from a bottle of cheap mescal that the bartender had sold them for two hits of Jack's mescaline. In the mountain town of Cuernavaca, we stopped at public urinals to piss. Half drunk, I had difficulty getting through the thick smell of stale beer and urine when it was my turn. The outhouse smelled like Vietnam, so I pretended a sniper watched me and I would die if I didn't enter the building. It worked. Next to the urinals, flies fought with mangy dogs for the right to occupy immaculate space in the shade of a huge cathedral.

Jack and I walked up the stone steps and into the building. Three brown dogs followed. "Ever see a dog trip?" Jack held out a white tab, and the lead dog lapped it up with his tongue as if it was a communion wafer. Jack was philanthropic about his drugs, the way a conch shell shares emptiness with an echo of the ocean. I truly believed Jack's smile was painted by Dali.

I soaked my fingers in the marble bowl beside the main entrance, like my ex-wife had taught me three years earlier. I had gone back to college after being discharged from the marines in the summer of 1969 and quickly became involved in the antiwar movement. I offered them an icon of a war gone bad and the movement offered me sanctuary and pseudo-absolution. I grew my hair long, got addicted to speed, and joined Vietnam Veterans Against the War. Becky approached me at a rally one night after I made a speech against the draft law, shouting at the top of my lungs, "An unjust law is no law at all." I developed as her new project. She acquainted me with various hallucinogenic drugs and the rituals of Catholicism. I acquainted her with the fear of intimacy. After a few months and with quiet resignation, Becky left me to study psychology. I left her to go somewhere I'd never been, the Catskill Mountains in New York, where I loafed my life away in Basil's Deli playing gin rummy for pennies and nickels with the locals.

The holy water on the tips of my fingers felt cold and dead, like the inside of my brain. Making the sign of the cross, the sacred wetness dripped over my forehead and onto my tie-dyed tee shirt. An old mantra Mac Barnett used to chant before patrols danced across my mind with each stroke of the fingers, "In thenameof the fatherson aaand holyspirit—IbetIcanbeatyou aaaat dominoes." The stained glass in the vestibule of the building was magnificent. I watched the life and death of Jesus unfold in lead-soldered strips of deep blue, purple, red, gold, and green glass around the upper walls. Sunlight poured through the glass and onto the open floor in a fantastic array of colors, as if some unseen hand had just turned a child's kaleidoscope and spilled the tiny crystals indiscriminately across the tiles.

Above the heavy wooden doors that Jack pushed open into the nave of the church there was a glass pane in the shape of a swan. The swan held a gold crown and banner in its bill with a Latin phrase inscribed across it. I didn't recognize any of the words because Latin was a dead language. Then I remembered one phrase of Latin from a poem I'd read in Joe Britton's British lit class, "The old lie: dulce et decorum est pro patria mori." What did that mean? Oh yeah—the idea that it was glorious to die for one's country was a big fat lie. Dying wasn't glorious, no matter who you did it for.

Standing now in the church at Cuernavaca, four years after my tour of duty in combat, I thought that maybe, just maybe, old poets were smarter than easily fooled young men. Maybe all old poets had once been easily fooled young men. Latin was truly a dead language, not because no one spoke it anymore, but because when you read the clever little inscriptions, you were encouraged to die. What did it matter if the dead people you remembered had names like Rick Santos or Mike Rawlings or Bobby Wolfe or Jesus Christ? They died because someone somewhere had written a lie in a language whose words were already dead—Semper Fidelis!

A slight breeze sighed through the open doors and tripped lightly along the balcony of the triforium, a sigh from God. Inside, the ceiling vaulted skyward, ribbed with iron supports. Painted angels gazed down at parishioners. I groaned with the weight of their absent eyes, like the clerestory directly above me groaned with the weight of heaven itself. Oh, there were icons blessed by some pope surrounding me, an altar inlaid with intricate mosaics carved in Aztec gold, rows of flickering candles, and a reliquary that contained a small fragment of bone. How the hell did a Catholic priest in Mexico know for sure that a yellow bit of calcium belonged to the petrified body of some human martyred five hundred years before and ten thousand miles away? How many times had I picked up body parts after an artillery attack and couldn't make the pieces fit the corpses? This cathedral symbolized a leap of faith I wanted to make, but couldn't.

Rising behind the altar itself was a huge boxlike structure. On the wooden shelves hand-carved statues of Bible figures rose almost sixty feet in the air, staring at me in guilty silence. The cloying scent of lilacs, old varnish, and candle wax hung in the air around an unhappy Jesus suspended on wire above the altar. Golden candlesticks surrounding the bishop's chair in the apse of the church shimmered and danced in the reflected light of a wide rose window. I genuflected, grabbed the wood railing that separated the altar from the front pews, and pulled my body up. The wood was cool and smooth to the touch, except for the small rounded arches carved beneath the railing. It seemed as if those arches were the gateways to a clean place somewhere behind the white curtain that draped the altar, a place I had grown much too dirty to enter. Because I was no longer blameless for man's inhumanity to man, but rather a participant in the game, and because I had the power to see ghosts, I swore that I even saw the lost innocence of several altar boys lurking in the shadows in both ends of the transept.

Something was still missing from the church at Cuernavaca. There were no mirrors, and rightly so. How can anyone hang a mirror in a place of sanctuary? Mirrors dissolve delusion. If this church had one, I might have been able to see who I really was, to remember a war I worked so hard continually to forget. It might have been the statue of the virgin or the hushed whispers of the two women covered with black shawls who genuflected before the altar, but suddenly I grew frightened. I had to leave, and at first, I didn't know why. Then I watched the old women kneel by rows of scented candles. One woman took a thin wooden stick, lit it, and touched the wick of a fresh candle. A small flame flickered. Blue heat, surrounded by an eerie yellow glow, rose from the wick.

What if the yellow flame was a human body and the blue core, the soul? It wasn't possible to extinguish the yellow without smothering the blue. Did that happen when you killed somebody? I looked away from the flame and shivered. I had to look again, and when I did, the shadows cast by the lit candle rustled along the walls, making the hagiographic mosaics shimmer and dance and come to life. Oh yes, the pictures in the candlelight told me a story all right, but it wasn't holy.

These old women reminded me with their lit candles that my soul was extinguished by the monsoons. The beauty of the artwork, the peaceful coolness of the marble columns, the baptismal font rising above the sculpted images of Satan where babies were cleansed, none of it brought me sanctuary from myself. Even the knowledge that some artist or architect may have donated his entire life to creating this place in such a way that the most horrific of sinners could find redemption was no comfort. The holiness that surrounded me just kept reminding me of my own evil. The perfect building made me remember that I was flawed. Men built a perfect form to praise a God that built imperfect ones.

"We gotta get out of here."

"Why?" asked Jack. "It's the only shady spot in town, and besides, I like the red and purple traces when those weird ladies light candles."

"Where's Basil?"

"Still pissing. He wants his wife to think he's got prostate cancer so she'll be sympathetic when he screws up, so he takes a long time to pee. It's like a symptom or something."

"His wife's four thousand miles from here. She has no idea how long it takes him to drain his dragon, you ignorant bastard. Besides, he's only a few years older that me. He's too young to have prostate problems. Go hurry him up. I got to get out of here now."

"Jesus."

*   *   *

The highway melted along a pearl beach into a ribbon of jet-set stores, juke joints, American fast food restaurants, and a few forlorn taco stands. With the cruise ship Klaxons and car horns blowing, the street vendors and tour guides screaming, and the faint rattle of a mariachi band, Acapulco seemed like a John Coltrane song composed of concrete and sand—discordance with purpose, clarity in confusion. We parked the Olds in front of an expensive-looking department store called Sandborn's. It hissed in anger at being left in the hot sun. When they had left Cuernavaca, Jack and Basil assumed we would stop somewhere for sleep, but, like a shark swims constantly to stay alive, I was in perpetual motion. Driving for hours was no sacrifice for a man convinced that something was about to be awakened inside him that was better left asleep. Ever since leaving Vietnam, I had felt like my intellect was on fire, that I needed to learn so much about everything in so little time. But, my emotions were full of novocaine and being extracted one by one. The candles in the church at Cuernavaca had caused a tingle of pain like the novocaine might be wearing off.

"Now what?" said Basil.

"We're here. Let's go in this place and check out the action." I pulled a Spanish dictionary from my back pocket and locked the car door.

"Do you really believe a department store is the liveliest spot in this town?"

"Hey, I hang out in the women's clothing section at Wal-Mart all the time," said Jack. "That is, until security runs me off."

"Look, this is somewhere I've never been. I know there's nothing waiting for me where I've already been. So humor me, okay?"

Pushing the glass door open, we three grubby-looking travelers walked past throngs of brightly colored tourists. They were mostly female, a produce market of tanned flesh.

"I'm hungry."

"Me too."

"I'm pretty much always hungry."

Around a rack of bathing suits, in the dining area, she sat eating a grapefruit covered with chili powder. I took it for a sign, a prophecy of sweetness and fire. Sweat gathered in my palms. I moved to the table where she laughed in chorus with an older woman.

"I guess it would be too much of a miracle if you spoke English."

"I speak it when I want to. What do you want?"

"I was going to say that I've never seen anyone eat fruit with chili powder."

"Then you haven't spent much time in Mexico."

"No, not much."

"Was there something else?"

"Probably. But . . . ."

"Let us try and move along. My time is running short. You can call me Rose. My name is Roceria but Rose will be easier for you. I am a secretary for an American company in Mexico City and I am here on a three-day holiday. I have a boyfriend who I will probably marry that beats me when he gets drunk because I make more money than him. When he is sober, he loves me for the same reason. This giggling person beside me is my mother. She speaks no English, so I can say what I want. So far, I am very bored and I am leaving tomorrow. I like your long hair and the earring. You look like a pirate. Would you like to make love before I go home, have six kids, and get fat?"

Rose stopped talking abruptly, as if she had finished reading a page and couldn't find the next one. I guessed a reply would have been in order, but there are moments in life when only silence is adequate. For example, the mind is silent when it dreams. I had been drinking so much tequila, had been so long without sleep, had been so shaken by the shadows in the cathedral that I had no idea if this beautiful woman actually spoke any of the words I'd just heard, and actually, I didn't really care. I felt grateful to be standing in front of her, trapped in her black eyes, reflecting her curiosity and desire, even if it was only a dream. The gratitude rose like an erection to fill Gloria Steinem and all the feminist pioneers who had taught women in the 1960s that they could control their own destinies, that men could be objects, used for pleasure and discarded at will. Sex was an expression of independence. Sex was a handshake, just a way to say hello. "Hello Rose. Use me," I said, and she stared at me, puzzled.

Fighting an urge to run back to Basil and Jack, I walked like a lost child.

"So," I said, trying to control the testosterone in my blood that threatened to erupt as an excited giggle. "We're staying at the El Mirador, right?"

"You got lucky with that beautiful, stupid, young woman?" asked Basil. "She probably doesn't even speak English and thinks you're Mick Jagger with those big fat lips of yours."

"Her name is Rose and she speaks the language of love. It's universal. Anyway, I need to meet you later. Rose is going to show me some things of interest. It might take awhile."

"I'd say about a minute and a half, if you concentrate on the 1969 World Series. Less than a minute otherwise."

Jack raised his drooping head and opened his glazed blue eyes with Basil's last comment. "You want some of my stay-awake medicine? It's also really good stay up medicine for those of us who feel limp frequently. Hey, and it'll make her face like Playdough in your brain. You can see Gracie Slick or Faye Dunaway while you're getting laid."

Rose owned a Volkswagen bus. When she and I left her mother at Sandborn's, the old lady just kept laughing into her cafe con leche. Driving along the highway that ran parallel to the beach, the girl seemed frightened and sad as we passed a new McDonald's and a Pizza Hut against a backdrop of beach huts and white sand.

"Once in my country, matadors, jai alai and agave worms were more than simple tourist attractions. We weren't all whores for the gringo dollars. We were real people. Our heritage has become just another selling point. It makes me sick. I hope for me that survival never becomes a stronger force than faith and dignity. I want to choose my own path, who I'm with, what I do, when I do it."

"We all feel that way at one time or another. Too bad. Sometimes we don't get to choose our paths, we just have to walk them."

She looked at me as if she no longer knew the English language and maneuvered the bus through traffic, turning left, turning right, then left again, in and out of a labyrinth-like neighborhood clustered with adobe apartments and cheap hotels. We stopped in front of a two-story yellow building. All the driving confused me. I knew it because climbing the stairs, I actually thought about what Rose had said and envied her naiveté. I thought about learning speech as a child. Each word formed a euphoria in my mind that rolled over my tongue like my grandmother's Christmas fudge. The more I learned, the greater my dependency on words became. Somewhere along the way in the jungles of Vietnam, I reached a point where there were only words and the words were impotent. Those same words I thought about before I enlisted, like *heritage, love, honor, faith, trust, dignity,* became various combinations of letters devoid of content.

On the other hand, Rose was an innocent. She still believed in something. A pilot flame of guilt began building inside me, and I remembered the old ladies in the cathedral lighting candles the day before. They believed in something also. Was I the only person in Mexico who believed in nothing? Was that the source of the overwhelming fear I felt when leaving Cuernavaca, the fear of being alone with myself, of being alone in the midst of people?

An hour later, the cheap hotel bed groaned. I stood up. Rose slept peacefully. From the balcony in her room, I could see two jeep loads of well-armed young Federales driving by on the street below. Their machine guns and olive-drab uniforms made me uneasy. This time it wasn't fear—it was pity. I felt sorry for the soldiers as they laughed with young laughter and lit cigarettes without knowing that their lives were out of their control. Dressing in the limbo of twilight, I walked from the room, downstairs, past the clerk, and into the quickening of night. I wanted to run as far away from Acapulco as possible just to be moving, but the thought of Rose's tongue, like Kama Sutra oil on my body, held me prisoner, made me sweat and dream along the noisy streets.

When I found the El Mirador and walked through the ornate lobby into the bar, the open-air veranda gave me a full view of the cove below and of the cliff diver. The diver climbed a hundred feet up the face of a sheer cliff. Spotlights followed. At the top, he knelt before an altar and a statue of the Virgin Mary, lighting more candles like the old women. This time the glow was reminding spectators of the man's willingness to risk life and limb for a few pesos and his faith that some unseen force protected his challenge of nature and saluted his courage. I thought of the story Father Lindeur told our CAG unit during the mass that Sunday before the Tet Offensive. It seems that Satan had tempted Jesus to take a chance and jump off a cliff. If he hit the rocks below and lived to talk about it, then everyone would know that God was his father. But Jesus had been smart enough to walk away, saying that his father shouldn't be put to a test. Pretty smart thinking. He got to put Satan in his place and not kill himself in the process. Of course, the Marine Corps was my father and Satan, not God. I had already jumped off my cliff.

The diver turned and dove into a small pool of seawater. One wrong twist, one mistimed move while the surf was sucked out into the mouth of the ocean, and the jagged rocks would be stained with machismo blood. I ordered a shot of tequila. I ordered another. After my fifth shot, I wanted to join him, light the candles, offer prayers, kiss the altar, and leap headlong into a net of warm air, pulled downward by the gravity of Rose's eyes. Breaking the surface of the jade water, I would flutter near the sandy bottom, until the reality of motion mingled with the illusion of death and forced me toward the surface.

I wanted to join him, but didn't. I looked at the altar and the image of the old ladies lighting candles in the cathedral at Cuernavaca rushed into my mind. I looked away and then back. They came into my mind again. They knelt there. Their heads were bowed and covered in black lace scarves. The sculpted figures set in relief along the cathedral walls seemed to bless the old women as they prayed.

My mind was playing tricks on me, as it sometimes did if I got too high. I wasn't in the cathedral. I sat in the El Mirador hotel bar, trying to get drunk. No old women prayed on the cliffside and still the diver hit the water safely. The crowd applauded. I ordered another shot of tequila and looked at the empty barstool next to mine just to make sure Rick hadn't come back. I could almost feel him in the room.

Stumbling up the stairs to my hotel room, I saw him in the long shadowed hallway motioning for me to come near. I took a step and leaned against the wall. The wet wood wept with these words—in all cathedrals all the dead are joined with all the living by memory and pain and inspiration and art. Maybe I could sleep through the whole night with the idea that it was possible in the carved stones of every temple to find forgiveness. Accepting that possibility brought me a temporary sort of peace.

Chapter 16

THE MIDNIGHT RIDER

Before my Mexican road trip, I returned to Kentucky Wesleyan College in September 1969. Two short years and whole worlds had passed. Besides the fact my left leg was filled with shrapnel and ached every day, on top of nights filled with sweating and horrific dreams, beyond my inability to focus on a functioning daily routine, I seemed to have landed on a different planet. My fraternity still existed, but it was no longer populated with beer-swilling rah-rah boys whose only motivations for going to college were to evade the draft and drink from kegs rather than cans. Most of those young men had flunked out like me and been drafted, or graduated and been drafted. A few lucky ones found open spots in postgraduate theological seminaries. Not even the federal government dared draft a fortunate son, future minister of God.

The fraternity house I moved back into echoed with the discordant mingling of twangy terror produced by Jimi Hendrix and his wa-wa pedal and the soft, but urgent, whining of Joan Baez singing "Blowing in the Wind." Rivers of smoke drifted from under closed doors. Sometimes the whole three-story house smelled like jasmine incense and other times like burnt tea leaves. Sometimes it seemed as if the joints being toked were so mellow the house might rise off its foundation and float into the sky.

Other times the house took on an angry edge when Petey or Joe scored a bag full of amphetamines or several lines of crystal meth. The acid, psilocybin, and mescaline disappeared frequently from candy dishes placed strategically throughout the upper two floors. Garbage bags rattled and clanked with empty bottles that once held Ripple, Bali Hai, Mad Dog 20/20, and a new antifreeze-based swill called Boone's Farm.

Attractive, intelligent women, high on freedom and good hash, came and went constantly performing acrobatic sex, often without even asking your name.

Initially, my fraternity brothers treated me with fear and loathing. Some thought I might be a government narc sent by the FBI to ruin their collegial utopia; others believed I hovered near the serial killer realm and could snap at any given moment, slaughtering them all like cattle in their sleep. Such was the climate of misunderstanding between those who came home from Vietnam and those who vowed never to go. That first semester the confusion and displacement almost drove me over the edge and into a nervous breakdown. I wanted desperately to belong to something. I had returned from war alienated from all human emotions except fear, loneliness, and guilt, my prewar values shattered by the knowledge that random violence was now all around me and in me no matter where I went. Death had become the frame that surrounded my life.

Yes, I needed to belong to something, and even this scruffy cluster of paranoid, hedonistic draft evaders and drug dealers would do. They would do because they were the opposite of the culture that caused me so much anguish and they were all I had. Within a few months, my hair grew halfway down my back. A beautiful, drunken young woman that I loved pierced my ear by placing an ice cube from her gin and tonic against the back of my left earlobe and ramming a darning needle through the flesh. A gold earring dangled in my left ear, and a desire to be constantly high, particularly on speed, in the presence of other humans dominated my days and nights. Snorting crystal meth or swallowing a handful of black beauties lifted me close to the adrenaline rush I had grown addicted to in the jungles of Vietnam.

I quickly became an accepted member of the new counterculture because I was willing to outdo them all in everything they did to prove myself. Still, it wasn't enough for me to forget who I was or what I had just done in the jungles of Southeast Asia. Only when I began to drop acid in the evenings as I crashed from speed did I find the altered state I searched for, until it both destroyed and regenerated my psyche.

One particular evening in 1970—I can't even remember when exactly—my friend Todd brought by some particularly potent red tablets of LSD. We split one tab and the other four people in my apartment split the rest. No one knew in those days that, when abused, amphetamine sulfate and all its derivatives created mock symptoms of an actual mental disorder, paranoid schizophrenia. Even if we knew, we wouldn't have noticed while we were high anyway.

I was crashing fast off the speed when the acid kicked in. The first few hours of bright colors, reverberating sounds, and animated traces of movement in the air caused laughter all around the room. I reveled in the feeling of oneness with my companions, as if I were inside them and part of them. I frolicked with the gods and melted into the stars that I thought actually were visible *through* my roof. Somewhere in the middle of becoming stardust the acid began to peak along with the paranoia, and the trip went sideways.

The wall in the living room collapsed, and on the other side, instead of my bedroom, was Vietnam. The hallucination swallowed me immediately like quicksand. Body parts covered the floor. Tracer rounds shot by my head. I ducked, bounced, hid behind the couch. The smell of cordite and gunpowder filled the air. Men screamed. I watched Todd as the top of his head blew off and what was left of his face became the face of Rick Santos. Covering my head with my hands, I screamed, "Incoming," and couldn't stop.

Obviously, screams were an unwanted distraction in an apartment building where the walls were made of sheetrock as thin as skin on the forehead. I rapidly became unmanageable. In their desire to keep the police away from the door, Todd and my other friends fed me several Seconal capsules. Being a powerful barbiturate, the Seconal quieted me. I was escorted to my bed, where I writhed and sweated for hours as the chemicals in my bloodstream fought each other for control of my mind. I suppose I could have died, but all I did finally was fall into a peaceful sleep. I specifically remember the dreams because there were no people or concrete images in them, only crystalline pieces of bright colors, as if someone turned a kaleidoscope in my brain.

When I finally woke up, twenty hours had passed. It was twilight of the next day and I lay in my bed alone. Dusky, grey light filtered in through the windows. I seemed to be in limbo, some purgatory between life and death, sanity and madness, peace and war. I walked from my bed to the mirror, gazing with wonder at the apparition I faced. My skin gave off a grey glow like the light in the room. For the longest time, I couldn't tell which image was real, the one in the mirror or the one staring at it.

A terror deeper and darker than anything I had experienced in combat leaked up through my subconscious and seeped into my consciousness like dirty oil. No more excuses like I had made to myself in the hospital in Japan when I saw Rick's memory come to life. For the first time, I accepted the possibility that I had lost control of my senses. I had gone crazy—really, uselessly, hopelessly insane.

Almost two years went by, two years with people's faces distorting if I looked directly at them, two years with phones and clocks reversing their numbers, two years getting out of bed at fifteen-minute intervals to see if the doors were locked, and two years trapped in a fear-adrenaline-fear syndrome that tried to kill me. How did I survive those months of misery? The same way I've survived the last thirty years—by throwing myself full force into one project after another. First, I joined Vietnam Veterans Against the War. Marching and speaking at rallies whenever and wherever I could, I performed some small psychic penance for my sins in Vietnam and for living through them. When no absolution came, I moved to New York and tried my hand at social work. As a recreational therapist who taught Bowery bums the value of making ceramic ashtrays, I learned from them that drinking could be contagious. So I left the detox ward and moved to the Catskills, where I got a job breaking horses to the saddle for trail riding in the mountains. There I met Basil and Jack and traveled to Mexico.

* * *

I'd like to tell you that after I cleaned the drugs from my system my life worked out perfect, or maybe, after my epiphany in Mexico I was cured of my psychic disturbances, like a little salve might cure a dog of mange. Then, those of you who feel the need, no matter how good your intentions may seem at the time, to send young people into preemptive wars for the sake of capitalism and the old puritanical "city on the hill" myth, could salve your own consciences even more than you already do. I'd like to tell you these things, but I seem compelled to tell you the truth.

I have fought my demons for thirty years. I may write another book about it someday. I tried my hand at half a dozen careers and four marriages. Somehow, I managed to raise two beautiful children and not damage them terribly. But until I accepted the facts that war, particularly this war, had altered forever the way I perceived the world, had made me into someone I couldn't always like, had caused me to redefine what it meant to be human, and that I was responsible for my own actions, having joined the Marine Corps of my own free will, I could not begin to heal. War is my car wreck every day.

I suspect that this is true of millions of American soldiers who managed to escape the killing fields of Vietnam with their lives, however frightened they may be to admit it. I suspect wars will continue because politicians start them and don't have to fight them. Ultimately, they are good for big business. I suspect there will always be young men and women willing to sacrifice lives, their own and others, for abstract and untenable concepts that sound glorious. I suspect each new American generation will create its veterans who are both victims and villains just like me. Consider our current effort in Iraq.

Ultimately, I suspect that I will continue to wake routinely from a restless and fragile sleep and feel sad.

YOU CAN'T GO HOME AGAIN

When Thomas Wolfe uttered his famous line so many years ago, he obviously meant a lot more than a geographical location. Home is that Holy Grail spot located within the stream of time when you found your *self*, when you finally understood that you were an independent entity operating your life by the exercise of free will, devoid of anything beyond the need to live life to the fullest, to gather an encyclopedic frame of reference for future living through your senses. This is the one time that you can smell the chemical makeup of air right before a rain, feel stardust sift through the clouds and settle on your skin, taste sunlight, hear a bird sing before it actually does, and see the colors of night. It is the moment you are most alive in the presence of death, when Garcia Lorca's *duende* fills your body like an artesian spring bubbling who you are from the inside out, rather than soaking up who you are from the outside in.

For me, home was in the jungles of Vietnam, the one place where life was at its best and worst simultaneously every minute of every day.

When I began telling you my story, the thought of going *home* never entered my mind. Quite the contrary—I had spent my life trying to forget the very place that made me, for better or worse, who I am today. I buried the questions in life that drive us all to do more than just get out of bed every morning, the need to understand why we are who we are, what makes us take a job at the local factory, marry our childhood sweetheart, divorce our childhood sweetheart, drink too much, love too little, love too much, go to church, stay away from church and curse God; what makes us romanticize war, why we choose one path instead of another, and what the choices we've made in the past mean for our future.

I'm not trying to make a case here that we live with those questions billboarded in our conscious mind, ever present in a static group of images and language. I'm saying that the questions exists within us like shadows, changing shape and form in direct correlation to the amount and angle of light we let in. However, some Native Americans believe that during Indian summer shadows gain substance and eat the soul. At some point during the last few years, I came to feel like this had begun to happen for me.

This is the Indian summer of my life. At the age of fifty-seven, it's my October, but it's also hot. Most days I wake up on fire with life and at the same time realize the blaze has limited fuel left to burn. I didn't want these shadows of questions to weaken the blue intensity of the flame.

The trip back to Vietnam that I made in August 2005 seemed to be the only real way of ending this book and coming to terms with who I am. It was a trip set in motion, albeit unconsciously, by the very first effort I made to translate the experience of my life into language, when I copied down on paper the quote from Ion Eremia recorded in the first chapter—"You must not silence that voice within you that is crying to be heard, or, as you yourself sense, there will always be a part of you that will remain unfulfilled."

As I wrote I kept hearing that voice and so, found myself planning, or perhaps a better phrase might be "spontaneously organizing," this trip. The first, almost insurmountable, obstacle for a poor poet and teacher was money. Plane fare from Evansville, Indiana, to Ho Chi Minh City (Saigon) cost a month's salary, and that was before I even started making hotel reservations, paying for malaria medicine and immunizations, booking in-country guides and transportation, and purchasing visas, along with the practical items necessary for a trip of this nature—aspirins, cala-mine lotion, writing paper, film, sunscreen, Neosporin, Band-Aids, hiking boots, and mosquito netting.

Fortunately, I work for a generous group of administrators at the University of Southern Indiana, people such as Linda Bennett, David Glassman, and Michael Aakhus, who sensed the value of this journey and encouraged me to pursue financing through the grant process. Then, the members of the Faculty Research and Creative Work Award committee had enough confidence in my ability as a writer to fund this project, especially considering the unorthodox nature of some requests. For example, how would it be possible to write off several hundred dollars needed for bribing local officials, either with cash or goods, so I could get to the places I wanted to go? There was no question it would have to be done. Even the official Web sites I browsed for Vietnam indicated that bribery was an accepted part of daily life for policemen and officials. With sala-ries being so low, who could blame them for supplementing their incomes via the foreign tourist trade? The phrase that finally satis-fied the accounting office and made those expenditures legitimate was "expediting conduits for services rendered."

There were issues well beyond the tangible for consideration. The primary issue, of course, centered on my emotional well-being. For three decades, I've dealt with a disorder common to most combat veterans raised in the Judeo-Christian tradition since the days of Imperial Rome. It's been labeled everything from "sol-dier's heart" to shell shock to the current phrase post-traumatic stress disorder. Millions of warriors have suffered from it, but it's always the same trouble sleeping, the same fear of intimacy, the same depression and survivor's guilt, the same tortured under-standing that war is an abomination, incomprehensibly evil and yet, incredibly exhilarating. It's almost like being bipolar at the same time. Finding the balance between hating what you did and loving the excitement it generated in your mind and body becomes a delicate, difficult, and long-term struggle. Go too far either way and you destroy yourself.

Beyond that, Christianity teaches you that killing is wrong, an almost unforgivable sin. Then, your Christian leaders send you forth to kill. Confusion attaches itself to your brain like one of those huge river leeches in the Mekong Delta and never lets go. You can no longer be completely sure of right and wrong, or completely trust the the people who run your society and establish the mores by which you're supposed to live. I had fought for my balance through four wives, a half-dozen or so careers, and a drug addiction. Would this trip reopen old scar tissue and make me a borderline dysfunctional old man, or would it heal my memories? I had to find out.

But I've become more cautious with age and learned that, whenever possible, it's best to stack the deck. So for the sake of some stability, I asked my twenty-three-year-old son, John, to travel with me rather than go alone. He's always been the adult in my family. Besides, he had just finished earning his master's degree in international relations, and a trip like this would help him translate theory into reality.

At 10 p.m. on August 2, 2005, we boarded Philippines Airlines Flight 103 from the Thomas Bradley International Terminal at Los Angeles International Airport after flying to Los Angeles early that same morning.

In the excitement of the day's activities, I had forgotten an important perspective required to deal successfully with life in Southeast Asia—the idea of an infinite reality. Past and future are simply shadows cast by and connected to the thick, muscular frame of the present tense. Even the Vietnamese language reflects this reality. There is no way to write any time but the here and now. Yes, like a beautiful woman, Time in Vietnam really fucks with your mind on several layers at once. After three and a half decades away from this phenomenon, I began to sense it again somewhere in the air between Hawaii and Guam.

It was black outside. An occasional star trickled across the cabin window like a fiery raindrop. We were eight miles above the ocean being propelled across the international dateline and into the future at six hundred miles an hour. I felt like I had been in limbo for weeks instead of a few hours.

Of course, this was my mind being tortured by Time with one of its favorite tools, boredom. I tried to fight back by reflecting on how the early explorers made this journey five hundred years ago following almost the exact route on the surface of the water instead of over it. It took them months, sometimes years, stopping at strategic ports along the way to cavort with the natives in a paradisiacal environment. I couldn't hold these thoughts for long, however, before memory began seeping around the edges of them.

I came to Vietnam the same way in 1967, on a Continental Airlines commercial passenger jet. In a matter of three days, I went from strolling through Frontier World at Disneyland in Anaheim, California, a small black-haired girl floating on my arm like a helium balloon, to running for my life as the mortar shells hit Da Nang airfield in South Vietnam. At least those early explorers had months on a ship to ignore the possibility of imminent death by sailing across the tranquil South China Sea instead of jetting over it.

My current flight had yet to land, but past, present, and future had begun already to fuse into one undistinguishable collective of memory, imagination, and reality.

*   *   *

Saigon at 3 a.m. I stared out a window from the ninth floor of the Grand Hotel. We had arrived at the airport in the early afternoon and taxied here. Below me, Nguyen Hue Boulevard slept in silence. A few hours ago, Nguyen Hue had been almost impossible to walk across. Hundreds upon hundreds of motor scooters and cyclos darted in and out between taxis, automobiles, and buses, often coming so close the riders would slap the fenders with open hands, signaling drivers to slow down or give way. A symphony of car horns blasted at different pitches with counterpoint harmony to the rising and falling rumble and buzz of various-sized exhaust pipes.

Diesel fuel mixed with ginger, sweat, fried pork, and the sludge floating in the Saigon River crowded my nose, not really blending into one discernible perfume, but fighting, as the city itself fought, for an identity—industrial, exotic, agrarian, urbane. Perhaps this was the yin and yang of all Southeast Asia.

But below my hotel window now in the early morning coolness of predawn, when the great cities of the capitalist world would have been awash in a sea of revelers, I witnessed the irony of a socialist state trying to maintain its principles while encouraging decadent money from Western society. All of the French-style boulevards in Saigon were deserted. Not even so much as a single delivery truck snuck down the wide lanes that were packed with people in the daylight. Nothing moved but an occasional stray cat and the palm tree leaves rustling in the monsoon breeze. It was still considered decadent by the government, as well as impractical, to waste the night fulfilling the desires of the flesh when the days required so much energy for the flesh just to survive.

Of course, not all citizens here in Saigon (I called it that because most of the city's residents still called it that) agreed with the government. There were places open all night in the back alleys and

Breakfast on the street, Hue.

the suburbs of Ho Chi Minh City that catered to almost every whim imaginable, from prepubescent prostitution to a pipe of opium. However, the current government maintained a policy quite different from so-called democratic governments held in place by the American military for the decades of the 1950s and 1960s. Back then, if you were caught indulging in one of these vices, you paid some petty South Vietnamese official a bribe and continued with your business. Under Communist rule, these types of so-called "victimless" crimes were punishable by a firing squad. The old adage—if you wanna play, you gotta pay—truly meant something more than words in modern-day Vietnam. On the morning of our arrival, we were met with the story of a European tourist on trial for his life because he got caught buying a twelve-year-old hooker.

* * *

The Bar des Amis, or the Place Where Friends Gather, was a small room located near the swimming pool on the first floor of our hotel. John and I found our way there for a drink on our first full day in Vietnam. Eight or ten tables spread out over the black tiled floor. A young waitress followed us to one and asked what we wanted. My son ordered a Tiger beer, which seemed simple enough because we had almost no command of her language and she had only a slight command of ours. I felt the need for a dry martini and asked for one straight up. Being polite, she left and returned with a light-complexioned bartender who bowed and asked me to repeat the order.

"Beefeater martini, straight up." He shook his head, not recognizing the label Beefeater. "Gin. You know gin."

"Stop being so condescending. You act like an American," said John. He was right. Why did Americans always assume that, no matter where we went, it became everyone else's problem to understand English rather than our responsibility to communicate in the native tongue?

"I know gin," the bartender said, "and I fix any drink you want. You want martini, I got martini." And I did get a martini, although on another occasion in the same bar I asked for Irish whiskey and received scotch. Any good Irishman will recognize the damage this does to the psyche.

The bar was almost deserted. Five other people, three white and two Asian, sat huddled around a small table in a dim corner of the room. I couldn't make out their conversation word for word because the tones were hushed and the distance too great. I did, however, catch enough to know the white men were American and they all discussed parallel elements of the Vietnam and Iraq wars. I don't mean they chatted about tactics and weapons or logistics and transport. They compared the effects of war on each generation of soldiers and civilians. I knew then that they were veterans, men who lived with death a single breath away every day for extended periods of time. War is never about *things* with us. It's always personal.

When the Vietnamese couple finished drinking bottled Coke, they disappeared into a room behind the bar. One of the Americans, a short, chunky, balding man in Levis and with faded tattoos streaming up and down both arms, approached our table.

"Name's Lenny. We'd like you to join us." He spoke with a thick Brooklyn accent and a slight nervous twitch of his upper lip. "I spent my time with the Americal Division. You?"

"How do you know I spent it with anybody?" I asked, as John and I moved to their table carefully, not wanting to spill our drinks and still cautious about our new friends.

"You got the look, for one thing. You got a cane for another, and you're American. Very few Americans come here just to vacation. It's too far from the States. So, you're either here on business, or you're looking for answers to questions that got raised a long time ago. You don't look like a businessman."

"I was with a Marine CAG up by Hue in I Corps area. Got hit during Tet of '68."

"Yeah. That was a rough one."

This was how I met Lenny, Spearman, and Noah in twenty-first-century Vietnam. This is how veterans from that war communicate with each other, in short, sharp spurts of memory and words like bursts of fire from an M-60 machine gun. I had nothing in common with any of these men, not neighborhoods, family, education, ethnicity (Spearman and Noah were African Americans), or purpose, nothing except that one event in our lives that made us brothers.

The three of them had been traveling back and forth to Vietnam together at least once a year for over a decade. On this occasion they planned to jump over into Cambodia and Laos for some sightseeing excursions. No matter how much they tried to justify the money and time they spent coming back, however, it soon became clear that, like me, they were driven by the need to feel whole, to be on the ground again in the place where guilt, imagination, memory, and morality had all fractured into separate pieces and only connected from time to time to irritate each other like distant cousins at an annual family reunion.

Spearman had been a medic during his tour and never got over the need to patch up the wounded.

"Fuck, I'm still working for the VA," he said. "I can't get past the fact that young people are still dying for politicians."

"We just made a trip to Walter Reed to visit with the guys coming back from Iraq. You talk about your bad wounds, man—these guys are fucked up. Arms—gone. Legs—gone. Faces—gone. Burned to shit. Blown away." Lenny lit a cigarette as he spoke.

"Don't forget their minds. They'll end up like us, mind-fucked," Noah softly offered.

My son gave me his "this guy isn't quite right look" from the other end of the table and I nodded in agreement. All of Noah's actions and words indicated, at least outwardly, that dark thoughts still existed continually in his conscious mind like nocturnal creatures that never really went away but hid in secluded corners well enough during the daylight to never be caught and removed. The VA shrinks called these "intrusive" thoughts. Some vets lived with more intrusion than others, and there seemed to be no rhyme or reason why. A guy could have been in a dozen firefights and be bothered only when certain stimuli occurred—helicopter rotors overhead; a hard, gray rain; a firecracker on the Fourth of July. Other guys may have seen no combat at all. They may have worked in the morgue or ferried bodies from the field or washed the blood from hospital operating floors. Yet the war replays itself constantly inside their heads, even after all these years.

"Here's what I don't get," Spearman said. "I talked to these soldiers coming back. I tried to help them see that this was just another politician's war for spoils, in this case oil. They get mad at me. They still believe Bush is a hero. They don't get it."

"Maybe they just need to believe their sacrifice was worth something." John looked at me when I spoke, reminding me of my penchant to get on my disillusioned romantic's soapbox, so I shut up.

"That really ain't too different from what we thought when we first came back. We wanted to make our actions right in our own minds," Lenny said.

"It didn't work though, did it?" Noah brought a poetic end to our talk.

*   *   *

The flight from Saigon to Hue reminded me of my childhood and the roller coaster at the Gibson County Fair. The old jet we flew in rattled profusely from the time we taxied down the runway until we landed. While the plastic and metal of the plane creaked, squealed, popped, and screamed, the crosscurrents from the Laotian and monsoon winds buffeted us up and down into peaks and valleys of air.

In less than two hours, we landed at the airstrip in Phu Bai, which had been a major resupply base for Marine Corps divisions operating in I Corps during the war. It was from here that I transferred to the village of Gia Le in the suburbs of Hue in 1967. The runway is still pockmarked with reminders of war and the terminal is the same concrete block building I remember.

Finally, I had arrived home. This was the place that began to smell like my Vietnam, the one that lives in my mind. I was *in country*. The fast-paced hustle and attempts at Western urbanity that defined Ho Chi Minh City had disappeared, replaced by wisps of wood smoke as the villagers lit their morning cook fires to heat pho noodles and broth for breakfast. Diesel fumes from old six-by trucks and slightly green wood on fire were the two constant smells I remember from Vietnam in the past. Strangely, I find the fact that both remain in reality the way they remain in my memory comforting, as if to say no matter what the rest of the world does to these villagers, their lives will continue in the same, slow, graceful way for eternity.

After hailing a taxi for the ten-mile ride to Hue, which has no airport, we turned north on Route 1. The shoulders of the road on both sides were much more cluttered with marketplaces, scooter repair shops, houses, huts, and Buddhist temples than they were during the American occupation. The villages that were relocated so war could be conducted in the 1960s had returned and, like the roadside between Phu Bai and Hue, had become cluttered with people. The tropical air soon became crowded with the scent of Asian life—mint, ginger, sesame, exotic flowers, and raw sewage from the Phu Cam Canal and the Perfume River.

The landscape had changed so much in the past thirty-seven years that nothing seemed familiar. Looking over the terrain that had once been as familiar to me as the neighborhoods of Princeton, Indiana, where I played as a child, I felt like any other tourist searching for unknown points of interest that might be worth a photograph.

"Look at that. What a mess," said John, leaning across the back seat of the taxi to try and snap a picture on my side of the road. "I bet it was beautiful once."

I followed the lens of his camera to a pile of rubble. All that remained of what obviously had been a Buddhist temple was the back wall and the Roman arch that served as a doorway. I recognized the damage and the artwork immediately, as if someone had flicked a switch and turned a bare lightbulb on in my brain—Rick Santos, satchel charges, blood and grey matter, shouts of horror, the shuffle of feet, and the stunning silence that always follows destruction.

"Goddamn it."

"What?"

"I blew that temple up. I'm in the middle of my old base camp. The government must have left it as some kind of reminder, which is ironic since both governments encourage your generation to forget." The temple site was roped off and signs marked it as some kind of cenotaph for fallen heroes.

"It's better economics to forget one war," John said. "That makes it easier to start a new one."

I couldn't help but see a small glimmer of hope in the fact that my son was at least aware of how history repeats itself. Knowledge is the first start toward understanding, and understanding is the first step toward the wisdom required to change.

*   *   *

The Huong Giang Hotel rose from the bank of the Perfume River, a monument to French colonialism both in décor and in the way Vietnamese valets and waiters hovered beside your elbow, hungry to please, as if not pleasing might bring them unmanageable misery and pain.

The hotel restaurant's dining area opened onto a wide veranda where we ate breakfast after a comfortable sleep our first full night in Hue. Long green tentacles of a vine dripped from an overhead lattice, stopping just short of our heads. The flowers that popped out of the stems at regular intervals were three shades of purple, beginning with a deep velvety shade and thinning by degrees to fragile lavender as the petals opened and fell away from the stamen.

As we sipped the famous Vietnamese drip coffee laced with thick, sweet condensed milk, huge bees, the biggest I've ever seen except for the John Belushi bee character on *Saturday Night Live* in the 1970s, dove into the flowers, buried their throats, and fed from the life force gathered in the centers. They buzzed within an inch of my head, but I felt no fear. The bees focused on one task and took no notice of my presence, content to live as nature required.

All the while, sampans motored by below us, churning the river into a cloud of mud and silt. Narrow skiffs glided across their wakes, barely skimming the water as the long paddles rose and dipped into it, powered by women in black pajamas and white conical hats. The women stopped working the oars only long enough

Citadel, Hue.

to take an occasional bite of rice from ceramic bowls placed in the bow. Then the work commenced again, as it had done in this efficient way for a thousand years.

This is one thing missing from my country, a blending of the natural and technological world. In America we fight nature as much as possible. Our cities struggle to remove wetlands so condominiums might replace them. Then we struggle with the damaged ecosystem and blame nature for our anguish. Our farmland is saturated with so many chemicals that black dirt now resembles gray ash and even earthworms refuse to live in it. But we'll harvest a few more bushels of grain per acre as the cancer rate climbs.

With all our wonderful scientific advancements, we have yet to learn that nature was meant to be our partner, not our slave.

*   *   *

The William Joiner Center for War and Social Consequences had given me the e-mail address of a Vietnamese poet who lived in Hue named Vo Que. The two of us communicated several times before I arrived and we made arrangements to meet on this morning of August 7, after John and I finished breakfast. When I reminded the desk clerk that I had an appointment, I told her the man's name and the time of our meeting. A look crossed her face similar to the expression of my daughter when she saw her first U2 video.

"You know Vo Que?" she asked, as if the idea was impossible.

"Yes. He's a poet who lives here."

"No, he's one of our *national* poets and Minister for Art and Literature. Everybody knows him. Mr. Vo Que is very important to our heritage."

"I am a poet also."

That simple statement made in Hue, which may have been wishful thinking on my part, brought me more respect and courtesy during my week there than if I had said I was a rock-and-roll star or a millionaire. What is cultivated in a society grows there, and the people of Hue cultivate art, literature, tradition, and human dignity. The more I began to realize this, the more regret filled my heart when I remembered the destruction wrought upon these gentle people by Communist and American forces during Tet. Who started it mattered less to me than how it ended—in the loss of innocent life and irreplaceable cultural artifacts.

Que arrived on his motor scooter a few minutes past eight o'clock. The morning sun and tropical humidity had already soaked us in sweat. He was a small man physically, maybe an inch or two shorter than me, and I'm barely five foot six inches. Que probably weighed no more than one hundred and thirty pounds, but his frame was wiry and he reminded me of a Siamese cat, quick, graceful, always balanced and ready to pounce. On the other hand, he exhibited those childlike qualities of innocent curiosity and joyful wonder for the life around him that made us, in our American arrogance and ignorance, see Vietnamese men as effeminate and weak. This gross misunderstanding caused us to underestimate their abilities as soldiers, which led to many unnecessary deaths on both sides.

Although Que spoke some English, he brought with him an interpreter named Y Nhi. Her mother and Que were close friends and Y Nhi worked as a translator for various government publications. She was also a highly respected musician, a graduate student in English literature at the university, and descended from ancient royal dynasties on both her mother and father's side of the family. Over the next few days she became an indispensable conduit for the exchange of ideas and memories that was to take place between two old poets.

Old patrol route, Ming Mang tombs.

"Mr. Vo Que says he is happy that you could visit our city under better circumstances."

"And I am honored that he shares his time with someone who was once an enemy," I said. She quickly translated my words. Que smiled, nodded, and off we went for the next four days to places I remembered as blood soaked and damaged seemingly beyond repair, like the Citadel and the Ming Mang tombs. Much had been restored, and these areas now overflowed with tourists from Japan, New Zealand, Australia, and several European countries on a regular basis.

At each of the stops, Que spoke eloquently of the rich Vietnamese heritage and struggle for independence dripping from stones and statues like the green moss. I learned about the Chinese influence, the French period of enslavement, and the American devastation from the perspective of a citizen, and not just any citizen, but one who had taken the experience of the last thousand years and translated it into poetry full of honor, wisdom, and dignity.

One of the surprising attitudes that prevailed most consistently after so many years was the intense loathing I noticed for the French. Considering the damage we did in our fifteen-year occupation, and the damage we were still doing through generational birth defects from Agent Orange, I would have thought that Americans deserved the brunt of ill will in Vietnam. Perhaps this feeling stemmed from my personal sense of guilt because it wasn't evident in the way we were being treated. So, when John and I wandered into a Hue back alley and through the door of the DMZ Bar for a beer, the sign on the wall—The French Suck Dead Dogs Dicks, Go Home Frenchman—struck me as graffiti worth exploring.

"The answer is simple," said Que over lunch at a place called the Garden Cafe. "The Americans came here to conquer us. We fought a war. The Vietnamese people understand war. It has been a way of life for us."

"But we did so much damage, destroyed so many lives . . ."

"Those are physical things. New people are born, new buildings are built, time heals the wounds for you and for us. The French enslaved us. They took our traditions, our heritage, and finally they wanted our humanity. This is a crime for which forgiveness is impossible."

When considered from that perspective, the concept of post-colonialism took on meaning for me beyond the literary label currently being applied to it in university English departments. The twenty-first century has become a time of multicultural reclamation, and we need to work hard as a nation at eliminating the fear and loathing of white male, Eurocentric domination so prevalent and well earned in the Third World, rather than rekindling it with broad strokes of American fatherly imperialism that for many people is indistinguishable from nineteenth-century colonial enslavement.

* * *

One of the things our military leaders during the Vietnam War failed to understand was the importance of the land to the Vietnamese people. To separate them from their land is to separate them from their souls. It's a concept that has always baffled the Western mind. For us, land is a tangible, negotiable commodity. It's to be bought and sold, conquered and traded away in treaties. The United States exists because of our willingness to believe this. But our willingness to believe this is the *only* way the ownership of land can be viewed has caused us to violate some of our own basic values in the past and will create similar moral dilemmas in our future. Consider the genocide of Native Americans as an example.

Peace ceremony.

When we began relocating South Vietnamese farmers to "strategic hamlets" and away from land their families had lived on for generations, like we did with Native Americans by moving them to reservations a century before, we lost all possibility of winning "hearts and minds" in South Vietnam, even if we would have fought the war for several more decades. I came to realize this when Que took us to dinner our last evening in Hue.

We had just concluded a formal peace ceremony at his office. The ceremony, simple and beautiful, consisted of our writing poems and reciting them to each other as a way to mend the spiritual scars between us. Y Nhi once again interpreted both ways while party officials looked on, stern yet pleased that two old warriors could make a new beginning. Then, we left the building and Que sealed our friendship by offering me a ride on the back of his scooter, an intimate and personal gesture, to an open-air café high in the hills above the city.

The owner of the café greeted us warmly. We were expected and treated like royalty. A waitress brought out a bucket stuffed with ice and bottles of Festival beer. Festival is brewed only in Hue from the water of the Perfume River. Next, a small grill, coals red and smoking, was placed in the center of the table along with a platter of raw pork. Through Y Nhi, Que explained: "This pig was raised and slaughtered right here in the village. By cooking it ourselves we bond with the villagers and share in their labor."

We wrapped the pork in mustard greens grown at the edge of the swamp next to the café and dipped it in salt that had been harvested from the nearby mountains, where a receding ancient sea had deposited it thousands of years before. After the pork, the waitress presented us with a pot of fish stew, which we laid across the grate on our grill to heat.

"This is a special fish," said Que, "caught from a warm spring nearby and given to us that way. It has been heated by the earth and when we cook and eat it, we will be bound to the natural world that gives the people of Hue life."

"How is it caught?" I asked.

"It's a rare fish and must be caught with the hair of a wise elder's beard twisted into a hook," Y Nhi said, and smiled as Vo Que snagged a silver hair from my beard. They both laughed like children at the startled expression on my son's face.

During the war, this whole area around Hue had been populated by refugee hamlets, peasants relocated away from their own land and living in perpetual isolation. Many of the trails I walked over during my visit were the same trails I had patrolled as a marine in the 1960s. I had joined the Combined Action Group because it gave me a sense of doing something worthwhile beyond the mindless killing. We thought we were protecting the noble but ignorant savages like any good and wise big brother would do. Instead, we turned them against us with our own ignorance, arrogance, and inconsideration of their way of life and right to live it. It seems to me this might be part of our current folly in the Middle East. Didn't George Santayana mention that those who refused to learn the lessons of history are doomed to repeat them?

After the meal, the owner of the place was called to our table and Que sang her a poem written particularly for this special occasion. The poem praised her talents as a chef, her commitment to the land, her poetic sensibilities, and her hospitality. I could tell she was greatly honored by Que's lavish praise. She laughed and bowed, and there was a certain spring added to her step when she walked away from our table.

Leaving a Citadel battleground.

* * *

Early the next morning, John and I took a taxi back to the Phu Bai airport and returned to Saigon, where we spent our last few days exploring the marketplaces, bars, and nightlife, hoping to soak up as much of this culture as possible before the long, exhausting trip home.

One afternoon in the Ben Thans market, a sprawling carnival of food booths, glass jewelry cases, electronic shops, clothing tents, and flower stalls, I was approached by a man about my age. Standing in the middle of morning glories surrounded by the odor of raw fish, this old soldier, with a plastic right arm and air where the left should have been, offered me a package of postcards. If I bought them, he told me, then he could help feed his family for the day, which would make him feel like a man again, and I could prove to all my friends that I visited Vietnam.

"This isn't my first trip," I said.

"You were here before the truce?"

I thought yes, before the truce, when his cracked teeth and my mind were whole, when the grass grew high watered with blood, when we were young men and truly believed there would always be enough rain for rice, when war seemed to be a necessary part of the greater good.

He placed the postcards in my palm. The metal clip on his prosthetic arm popped like a real knuckle, warm with flesh, might have done when releasing a weight. But the stainless steel hook was cold, and the curtain of pain drawn across his eyes told me nothing of how this man felt about not being able to caress his wife, pat his children on the head when they were little, or even work like the women in his village cultivating rice. It didn't occur to me to ask what side he had fought on.